SHE FOUND A WAY

From Sacrifice to Success—A First-Gen Story

Rosario Aranda

ALEgRíA PUBLISHING

Edited by: Anne Marie Wells
Author photo: Carla Perez, Besame Mucho Photography
Cover design: Diane Castaneda, Sirenas Creative

ISBN: 9798995625605

To my mother, my abuelitas, and every woman who came before me.

To first-gens who are breaking generational cycles and for the next generation, may you go further.

"It is a beautiful thing to be a First and Only, the one who disrupts deep-rooted generational patterns to become our ancestors' dreams. And it also comes at a price."

- Alejandra Campoverdi

Table of Contents

A Letter to You

There were so many days when I was juggling work, college, and caring for my mom, where I would sit alone in my car and cry. Sitting in the driver's seat of my parked car, I cried into the steering wheel. I had just gotten home after a day of working at a bank and going to community college. It was 10 PM, and my mother, who was homebound with kidney failure, was waiting for me to walk through the door. In those moments, I would whisper to myself, "How am I going to do this? How am I going to find a way?" The truth was, I didn't know. I felt overwhelmed, uncertain, and alone.

I didn't know anyone who was navigating what I was navigating. I searched for a story like mine in the library, a story of a daughter of immigrants who turned their parents' sacrifices and their own struggles into something meaningful.

As I got older, I started hearing other first-gen stories through social media and the internet. Each one was powerful, each one unique, and yet none of them felt exactly like mine. That's when I realized maybe the story I'd been searching for was the one I was living. Maybe the loneliness, the late nights, the tears in my car, and the struggles our family experienced weren't just obstacles. Maybe they were chapters being written in real time.

I began to see other Latinas sharing their stories and

writing books. I began to think that my journey had a purpose, that my voice mattered, and that there were other children of immigrants out there who needed to feel seen, understood, and reminded that they weren't alone either.

I also want you to see my story as proof that you can turn your parents' sacrifices and every obstacle placed in your path into your own version of success, that no matter what you're carrying, you will always find a way forward. And sometimes, when you feel lost or unsure, the way will find you.

That's what resilience looks like for us, for the daughters and sons, the first-gens, the children of dreamers who dared to believe in something better. We learn to rise even when the path is unclear. We learn to create opportunities out of moments that were meant to break us. And we learned that our parents' dreams didn't end with their sacrifices; they continue through our courage.

And so this is where my story truly begins, not with me, but with the countless sacrifices my parents made so that I could have a life filled with opportunities they never had. It begins with the small moments I witnessed as a child: the long hours, the evenings when they put everyone else first, their strength in the face of hardship. These pages are a tribute to their courage and to the journey.

As you begin to read, I hope these pages fill you with hope, determination, and inspiration, not because the journey is easy, but because it's possible. I hope you see pieces of your own story reflected here and feel less alone in the moments that feel heavy. And if you ever find yourself wondering, "How am I going to do this? How am I going to find a way?" I hope this book reminds you that even without all the answers, you are capable of moving forward, and that sometimes, the way will find you.

Chapter 1

The Weight of Their Dreams

At six o'clock in the evening, my dad would walk through the front door in his frayed-knee jeans and shirt stained with stucco, paint, and sweat, after a long day at the construction site. Relief would wash over his face after another full day of backbreaking labor. His calloused hands, still dusted with the grime of the day, would drop his tools by the door before entering the living room where he'd greet my older brother hunched over the coffee table, concentrating on his homework. Then my dad would come into the kitchen where six-year-old me would be standing by the counter, "helping" my mom prepare dinner. Those pink leggings I loved to wear would cling to my skinny flamingo legs, and my lips would be smeared with my mom's lipstick—a bold fuchsia that made me feel like a Disney princess, even if it was crooked and gaudy. I would clutch a wooden spoon like it were a magic wand, convinced I was my mom's sous-chef. The radio would play in the background, filling the room with the familiar sound of "La Puerta Negra" by Los Tigres del Norte, my favorite song at the time. Whenever it came on, I couldn't resist dancing across the kitchen, twirling and stomping to the beat. My mom would have just come home around 5 p.m. from her shift at the restaurant, still in her work clothes and tired from the day. She would hum along as she stirred a pot on the stove, pausing now and then to smile at me, her little girl in pink lipstick, spinning in the kitchen, giving her a moment of lightness at the end of a long day.

My dad would lean down to kiss me on the forehead and give my mom a tired and affectionate smile before setting his lunchbox on the counter with a heavy thud. The smell of dirt, sun, and sweat never seemed to loosen their grip from his skin.

Without saying more, he would head to the bathroom to shower, eager to wash the day away. This would be the first time I would see him all day. He always left for work before the sun came up, long before I had even opened my eyes for school.

My mom would be cooking, maybe preparing leftovers from the day before like carne en su jugo con frijoles, meat cooked in its own juices with beans, my dad's favorite. The rich aroma would fill the kitchen, blending with the radio and the clinking pots and pans.

I would help my mom set the table, arranging the plates, cups, and silverware just right. She would hand me warm tortillas wrapped in a kitchen towel, and I would place them at the center of the table. Then I would put the two-liter bottle of Coca-Cola on the table. That bottle always made even the simplest dinners feel like a special occasion.

When my dad came out of the bathroom, freshly showered and faintly smelling of baby oil, he would sit at the head of the table, the only seat with a clear view of the TV. He would grab the remote from its home on the coffee table and switch the channel to Univision for the evening news, sending the anchor's voice across the room as we would take our seats.

My mom would call my brother to eat, but it wouldn't be until my dad raised his voice that he would close his notebook and hurry to the table.

At the table, my dad would ask the same question he always did: "¿Cómo les fue en la escuela?" "How was school?" My brother and I would answer with our usual, "Bien." "Good." Then my dad would follow-up with "¿Y qué aprendieron?" "What did you learn?" My brother and I would look at each other and mutter the same answer as always: "Nada." "Nothing."

My dad would give us that serious look with furrowed brows and steady eyes that made us sit up a little straighter. He wouldn't say much as he ate, his attention shifting between the news and his plate. But we knew the speech we had heard countless times before was coming.

"Education is the key to your future. You need to study hard so you don't end up like me and your mom working long hours, sacrificing our bodies, our time, and our dreams so you can build better lives."

Those dinners were simple, but they contained more than just food. They held lessons, love, and the weight of two people's sacrifices, people who once were children with their own dreams.

My mom was only twelve years old when her mother, my abuela Rosario, died from an infected cat bite. Living in a small, humble house in a small town in Colima, Mexico, with chipped paint on the walls and no running hot water, my mom had no choice but to drop out of school to take care of her four younger siblings — the youngest just six months old. Her two older sisters were already married and managing their own homes, and her father worked long hours on a farm. So, she took on the role of a replacement mother and second provider.

She started by washing and ironing clothes for neighbors. With the small amount of money she earned, she bought formula and diapers for her baby brother.

In her early twenties, a cousin in Los Angeles called to tell her about job opportunities in the U.S. She romanticized the idea of heading north now that her younger siblings were old enough to care for each other, earning dollars instead of pesos, and saving for a sewing machine to open a tailoring shop back in her hometown. She didn't intend to stay forever, just long enough to give herself a shot at something more. She didn't realize her plans would change.

It was an early morning in April when she boarded a northbound bus, leaving Colima behind with only a backpack, 1,000 pesos (equal to about $600 in 2026), two changes of clothes wrapped in plastic, and a head full of dreams. It took her three days to reach Tijuana, where she met José, the coyote her cousin had arranged for her, who would help her and a handful of others cross the U.S. border.

José handed her an American ID with a woman's photo who looked similar. He told her to style her hair like the woman in the picture and to walk calmly across the border checkpoint, holding the ID by her shoulder. After crossing, she was to look like she was shopping at a nearby market to blend in while waiting for the rest of the group to cross. When everyone made it through, they jumped into a van and headed to Los Angeles.

There, her cousin was waiting for her. Her cousin had paid $325 (around $2,600 in 2026) for the crossing, which my mom later reimbursed. Her first job was as a live-in nanny for two children, earning $40 (about $300 in 2026) a week. After each paycheck, she sent half her earnings back to her siblings in Mexico. After two years, she left her nannying job and started building her own life. She moved in with her friend and got a job at a ceramic factory, making $1.50 (about $12 in 2026) an hour Monday through Friday. On weekends, she worked at a restaurant, earning $50 (about $400 in 2026) over eight full days of work and relying on tips to get by.

My dad, on the other hand, had just finished middle school when he decided to leave Mexico, just barely a teenager. My dad is one of twelve children, and when he was born, all fourteen of his family members lived in a two-bedroom, one-bathroom house outside Guadalajara. There was rarely enough food. Most days, they ate beans and tortillas. Sometimes, only beans.

Feeling responsible for helping the family, his oldest brother had moved to Santa Barbara to work as a cook in a restaurant. Soon after, my dad followed. He left school and home and never returned to Mexico. Even at the tender age of thirteen, his life focused on one goal: earning money and sending it home.

The journey took him three days by bus to Tijuana. There, he met a coyote arranged by his brother, who paid $300 for the crossing. One dark Tuesday night, the coyote led him and six others to a hole under the border fence. They waited until the Border Patrol switched shifts at midnight, then crawled through and ran a few miles to where a pickup truck was waiting. They jumped in, lay flat in the bed, and the driver threw a black tarp over them, told them to be silent, and then sped off. Two hours later, they arrived in a McDonald's parking lot somewhere in Los Angeles.
My uncle was already there waiting for him. The two brothers drove straight to Santa Barbara and within days, my dad got a job under the table as a dishwasher at the same restaurant where his brother worked.

It was the summer of 1978 when my parents met. My mom was walking to work, passing by a familiar house where my dad and his friends often hung out. She had noticed him before but had never spoken to him. That day, a small, scrappy dog began barking at her and wouldn't back off. She kept walking, hoping it would leave her alone, but the dog started tugging at the bell-bottoms of her jeans.

Just then, my dad stepped in. "¿Te está molestando el perro?" "Is the dog bothering you?" he asked as he tried to shoo the dog away. She laughed and nodded, grateful for the help. After finally chasing the little dog off, he struck up a conversation. Something about that moment sparked a connection.

Before she walked away, he invited her to join him and some friends for dinner and drinks that weekend. She said yes. That night turned into many more, and soon their relationship deepened. My mom soon found out she was pregnant with my brother. Although they never married, they continued to build their life together, and years later, their little family grew again, this time with me.

I was born in Boyle Heights, California where we spent the first couple of years of my life, years I don't remember but that shaped the foundation of who I would become.

They left everything behind so we would never have to. My mom never opened a tailoring business back in her hometown, and my dad never bought a farm. They gave up their dreams so that my brother and I could chase ours.

But chasing dreams as a first gen isn't as simple as it sounds. In each classroom I entered, along with my binders and textbooks, I carried the sacrifices of my parents and the dreams of my ancestors, the women who came before me who never had the opportunities I now held in the palm of my hand. I felt the pressure to prove that those ancestral barriers stacked against us could be broken. I knew my story was beginning from their resilience and strength that paved my way, and because I carried that weight with me, I also knew my story couldn't end with a high school diploma.

Chapter 2

Early Lessons

In 1990, our family moved to San Jose so my dad could join my uncle's construction business. We moved into a two-bedroom apartment with a private balcony. At home, I often heard, "No hay dinero". Even at five years old, this confused me because I saw how hard my parents worked. My dad worked long hours, leaving before sunrise and coming home in the evening covered in sweat, dirt and stucco. My mom was on her feet all day and she would complain about her feet hurting.

One of the things that kept money tight was their language barrier. They knew enough conversational English to get by, but without much free time to study or practice, they couldn't go much further. My brother and I took on adult tasks, like reading and translating important documents, attending doctors' appointments, filling out forms, and explaining letters from school. We became the link between our parents and the world, carrying a responsibility we didn't fully understand but knew was important.

After a long day at work, my parents would ask us to open the mail. I remember the silence that followed as my brother, and I would read the bills out loud. My mom or dad would sigh, showing worry on their faces. Sometimes, we'd come home from school and see a note from the landlord about overdue rent taped to the door. We would read it to them when they got home. They always answered the same way, looking tired but determined, saying, "El viernes lo pago ya que me paguen." "I'll pay it on Friday when I get paid." Followed by, "Dios aprieta pero no ahorca," or "God squeezes but does not strangle." A phrase they would say often during challenging times.

We only bought new things when we really needed them. My parents waited to buy me new shoes until my old ones were worn out with holes. Sometimes I felt embarrassed at school when I saw other kids with their spotless Nike or Adidas sneakers, while my Payless shoes were falling apart. Then I'd feel embarrassed to be embarrassed because I knew my parents always did their best to provide for us. We usually had what we needed, even if it wasn't always what we wanted.

While I watched my parents face their own struggles, I was dealing with my own, trying to fit in at school while staying true to my Mexican roots at home. Even my name felt like it belonged to two different worlds. I was named after my grandmother Rosario, who was strong and caring, but at school, teachers often mispronounced it. Even though I knew my name had meaning, and that I was a part of my grandmother, each time I was singled out, I wished I had an easier name like Lisa or Sara.

I was put in ESL classes where I met kids from Vietnam and Afghanistan. Even surrounded by different accents, not many spoke Spanish like me, and I often felt alone, carrying both worlds with me, Mexican at home and American at school. Trying to do both sometimes made me feel like I wasn't doing either very well.

Growing up in a low-income family meant I qualified for free school lunches which helped my parents worry less about money and let me try the same cafeteria food as everyone else. Besides, I didn't want to explain to my classmates what chile relleno (poblano peppers stuffed with cheese, dipped in an egg batter and fried until golden) was while they ate their Lunchables.

I never realized how different my life was until I was seven years old when I visited my friend Ashley's house. It was the first time my parents allowed me to go to a friend's home, and I was nervous but excited. My palms were damp as I smoothed them over my dress, reminding myself to be on my best behavior. When the door swung open, Ashley greeted me with her usual bubbly energy, her straight blonde hair neatly parted to the side and clipped back with a sparkly purple barrette. Her hair stopped on her shoulders and bounced slightly as she led me inside.

Her house felt massive, like something out of a movie. The carpet was soft and clean and family photos from vacations and school plays lined the walls. Was this how all Americans lived? In spotless homes where sunlight poured in through the windows and backyards opened to sparkling blue pools? I tried to hide my mesmerization, stealing glances through the glass door, wondering what it might feel like to swim in something that looked like a mermaid's home.

Ashley showed me her room with pride. Shelves of dolls lined the pastel pink walls. The dresser and nightstand of her matching bedroom set had little gold knobs, and her bed had sheer pink curtains that made it look like something from a fairytale. Stuffed animals filled one shelf and her trophies from dance recitals filled another. Could I ever bring Ashley to see my room that I shared with my brother? What would she think of our bunk beds, old blankets, and walls decorated not with posters or trophies, but with pictures of Jesús and La Virgen watching over us?

When Ashley's mom offered us juice boxes and snacks, she didn't ask Ashley to translate anything for her. In fact, Ashley never helped her parents fill out forms or translate overdue rent notices. She didn't have to explain doctor bills or interpret at parent-teacher conferences. Ashley's world looked so much easier, so much lighter. Her world was full of choices instead of responsibilities.

When I returned to my family's small apartment, the contrast felt even stronger. That visit showed me another way of living, one in which people lived in big houses with pools and children had their own rooms.

When I was eight, I came down with a bad sore throat and had to stay home from school. Without health insurance, anytime one of us got sick, we faced an added financial stress. Doctor's visits meant paying out of pocket, so we only went if it was absolutely necessary. No annual checkup. No x-ray for a twisted ankle. No wellness visits if we had the sniffles.

My parents had to scrape together $100 in cash so a doctor could diagnose me with tonsillitis. The American healthcare system wasn't designed for families like ours. Even with my aching, scratching throat, I still had to interpret between the doctor and my parents. After being prescribed antibiotics and told to rest, we left, and I stayed home from school that week.

My parents still had to work though. Missing a shift meant missing out on income they could not afford to lose. They never took time off unless there was no other option. And with no family or community to ask for help, I stayed home alone, sick, at eight years old.

I spent most of the time lying on the couch with a blanket, watching cartoons and reruns of old sitcoms. Eggo waffles became my go-to meal since they were easy to pop into the toaster. My mom would leave them on the counter with a plastic cup of orange juice before heading out for work. Before she left, she always reminded me to lock the doors and never open the door for anyone. "No abras la puerta, aunque toquen," she'd say. "Even if they knock."

Throughout the day, she would call the house to check on me. I'd run to answer the phone, happy to hear her voice.

"Mija, how are you feeling?" she would ask in Spanish.

"Okay," I'd say, trying to sound stronger than I felt.

"Did you take your medicine?"

"Yes."

"Okay. I'll call you again on my next break."

"Okay."

"I love you."

"I love you too."

Even from a distance, she found a way to care for me.

There were no Hispanic teachers at my elementary school, and the only adult who spoke some Spanish was the school nurse. So whenever my mom came to school for parent-teacher conferences, I had to speak for her, even though I sometimes doubted if I was saying things right. My dad could never come to these meetings because he worked long hours on construction sites around the Bay Area. He made it to after-school performances or events, when possible, but it was my mom who always found a way to be there.

Translating during meetings made me feel caught between two languages, never fully confident in either. I worried about making mistakes or missing something important. It left me feeling insecure, like I was struggling with something that seemed easy for other kids.

At my second-grade parent-teacher conference with Mrs. Stevens, I sat next to my mom in one of the small student chairs, my feet barely touching the floor. I couldn't sit still and kept fidgeting, nervous about what my teacher would say. It was even more stressful knowing I had to translate everything for my mom. Would there be something bad? Did I talk too much or not enough? As a shy kid, I always worried, but Mrs. Stevens only had kind things to say.

"She is a wonderful student," she began, smiling at me. "Very respectful and friendly with the other students."

I turned to my mom, my small voice steady but careful. "She says I'm a good student… and that I'm nice to others."

My mom asked, "Really?"

Mrs. Stevens nodded. "You should be very proud of her."

I smiled, translating again. "She says you should be proud of me."

As a kid, I knew how important it was for me to do well in school, to stay healthy, to keep tidy. I carried a burden to not further burden my parents by getting bad grades or getting sick or being messy. I had to do my part. When I was nine, though, I was getting ready for bed when I heard the muffled sound of crying from the bathroom. My dad and brother were in the living room, watching TV with the volume up, completely unaware, so I knew it had to be my mom. I tiptoed closer and placed my ear against the door, trying to be sure of what I was hearing. The door was unlocked, so I gently pushed it open and peeked inside. My mom was sitting on the closed toilet lid, elbows on her knees, face buried in her hands. She was crying in a way I had never seen before; deep, heavy sobs that made her body tremble. I slowly crawled into the room and sat at her feet, unsure what to say but needing to be near her.

"What's wrong, Mami?" I asked softly. She didn't respond. She continued to sob while I sat silently, hoping my presence would bring her some comfort.

"Mami? What's wrong?" I asked again, "I want to help you."

"You're too young to understand," she said through her tears.

I stroked her hair and rubbed her back in the gentle way she did for me when I was upset.

"Mami, I want to help you," I told her again.

"You can't," she whispered. "You won't understand this now," she said as her breathing slowed and tears eased, "but promise me you'll keep studying. Go to college. Get a good job, one that pays you well. Don't have children until you're able to feed them yourself. And never, ever depend on anyone."

"I promise, Mami."

Even though we faced a lot of challenges, my parents always tried to make happy memories for us. Some nights, I would sit with my mom and watch telenovelas, getting caught up in the stories. On Saturdays, we all gathered in front of the TV to watch *Sábado Gigante,* the longest-running Spanish variety show that aired for three hours on Saturday night.

The show had a mix of musical performances, interviews, and game contests that always ended in someone driving away in a new car. It was a staple in our house. The show brought so much laughter and excitement into our small living room. My brother, who was usually quiet, would sometimes do impressions of El Chacal or tell a quick joke during commercials, making us laugh without putting himself in the spotlight.

Sundays had a rhythm of their own. I would wake up to the music of Los Panchos on the radio, and we would all get ready to attend Sunday mass at the Cathedral Basilica of St. Joseph. After church, we'd sometimes head to La Pulga, the Berryessa Flea Market. It was crowded and full of life, with music blasting from speakers and the smell of grilled corn and tacos in the air. My brother and I would walk side by side, sometimes racing ahead of our parents to peek at video game booths or flip through boxes of used VHS tapes. My brother loved video games and would spend forever studying the covers before picking one. My parents always bought us a cup of French fries to share, my favorite, and my brother would usually let me take the last few even if he wanted them for himself. While we snacked, my mom would stock up on produce, and sometimes we'd shop for back-to-school clothes at the stalls. I never admitted it to my classmates, but many of my outfits came from the flea market.

On Sunday nights, my dad went to bed early to prepare for another long work week. My mom, brother, and I would stay up a little longer to watch *In Living Color.* We laughed together, especially at the silly and outrageous sketches with Fire Marshall Bill and Wanda. Despite the language barrier, my mom found joy in the humor. Watching her laugh at something not in her native tongue was its own kind of victory. It reminded me that joy, like love, could transcend language. My brother and I loved that show so much that even now, as adults, we bring up those memories and talk about how much we miss it. He can still quote the sketches word for word, and sometimes we slip back into the voices just to make each other laugh.

At home, food often brought our family together. On special days, my mom made pozole, one of my favorites, a traditional Mexican soup made with hominy, tender pork or chicken, and a rich red or green chili broth. I absolutely loved it, and it would fill the house with a comforting aroma that always meant celebration. Every year on my birthday, my mom would cook it for me because she knew how much I loved it. My brother always let me have the first bowl, even though he was just as eager to eat. While my mom kept our traditions going, she also tried to include the American ones we learned about at school. She started making Thanksgiving dinners, trying to copy the recipes she heard about from other families. Her stuffing never tasted quite like anyone else's, but to me, it was perfect because she made it.

By the time we moved to San Jose when I was five, my parents had become legal residents thanks to an amnesty program in the '80s, which meant we could visit family in Mexico. My parents tried to save as much as they could so we could visit during some school breaks. It wasn't always easy, and I'm not sure how they managed to do it, but they made it happen. Traveling there meant long and hot bus rides during the summer. When we arrived, we were always greeted with open arms, warm hugs, and homemade food. My brother and I had a blast playing with our cousins, running in the fields, playing fútbol in the streets, and staying up late listening to stories from the adults. Seeing how some of our relatives lived, though, without access to hot water or with a small home that accommodated two families, made us grateful for what we had in the U.S., even if it didn't always feel like much. What were the most important things in life anyway? Family? Connection? Joy? Love? Those don't cost a thing.

Maybe it was because we shared a similar struggle, but my brother and I were very close despite being six years apart. At school, whether I faced confusing homework or feelings of overwhelm, my brother would step up to help me with multiplication tables. As the older sibling, he naturally assumed a protective role. I looked up to him, not just because he was older, but because he carried so much without seeking attention or praise. His calm, loving presence left a deep impression on me. What I didn't realize at the time was that his protective instinct would eventually take him far from home. The strength I admired in him would guide him toward a future I wasn't prepared for: the military.

Chapter 3

Raised on Responsibility

By the time I reached middle school, life at home began to shift in a way I hadn't expected. My brother graduated from high school and decided to join the Marine Corps. My parents weren't thrilled. Military service is inherently dangerous, but they respected his choice. He was becoming a man and needed to carve out his own path.

For me, his departure felt like losing a part of my foundation. I was proud of him but also scared. I couldn't help but worry about what he might face in the world. Plus, up until that point, my brother and I had always shared the responsibility of being the bridge for our parents—translating, interpreting, filling out paperwork, and helping them navigate a world they hadn't grown up in. He was the one who filled out their DMV forms, explained bills, or called the cable company when something went wrong. He handled it all calmly and without complaint. When I didn't understand something, I could count on him to explain it to me first, before we had to explain it to them. With him gone, that role now fell entirely on me alone. I felt a little bit abandoned.

Looking back, though, I realize my brother saw the military not as an escape route from our family, but as an entrance into the wider world beyond what any of us knew. He was always the reserved, observant one, but there was firm determination in him. Though he never voiced it, I sensed the heavy burden he carried of being the eldest child. He faltered between his desire to safeguard us and his desire to do something that would make our family proud, even if we didn't understand his choices initially.

Without my brother, I suddenly felt older even though I was still a preteen. The longer he was away, the more the silence at home grew heavier and more somber. I missed how my brother would make me laugh with his sarcastic comments. I missed watching him play video games and even missed begging him for a turn. He'd often ignore me at first, but soon he'd give me the controller and sit beside me, helping me through each level.

His absence marked the beginning of a new chapter for me, one where I had to step into shoes that still felt too big and take on more responsibility than most kids my age. But even from afar, I carried the example he left behind: steady, calm, dependable. That part of him never left.

In middle school, I made new friends and was happy to see a couple of my cousins there too, it helped me feel like I belonged a little more. For the first time, I also had a Latino teacher who spoke Spanish: Mr. Ramos. He always stood outside his door with a smile and greeted us as we walked in. He would joke around in class and never raised his voice. He was warm, funny, and deeply passionate about his work. Everyone loved him. He had a huge heart and a presence that made every student feel seen, especially

Latino students. When we talked, we communicated in Spanglish. Watching him take pride in who he was and where he came from made me think more often about attending college.

Middle school was also when I began caring more about my appearance and following the trends of that era like wearing lip liner but no lipstick, plucking my eyebrows, and using Aqua Net hairspray. I tried to stay up to date with fashion, sporting bell-bottom jeans and tops from Forever 21. These small experiments with style and self-expression became my way of testing the waters of adolescence while still navigating the expectations and limitations of home.

I remembered my parents' constant reminders to study hard, and I took their words seriously. I tried my best to do well in school by turning in my assignments on time and staying up late to study. I wasn't a straight-A student, but I consistently did above-average work and took pride in doing my best.

In high school, I met more Latino students, which made school feel more relatable and less isolating. It was also the first time I seriously thought about life after high school. Our teachers often talked about different career paths, and I felt overwhelmed by at the possibilities. Maybe I should be a nurse? But could I also be a social worker or teacher? When I sat down with my school counselor, she told me I had the potential to go to a four-year university.

"You have good grades, Rosario," she said, her voice warm and steady. "I really think you could thrive at a university.

Have you thought about applying?"

Rather than feeling excited, I felt a knot tighten in my stomach. My cheeks felt warm as I nodded politely, forcing a small smile.

"Yeah... maybe," I murmured.

Inside my chest, a wave of panic rose. I couldn't imagine asking my parents to take on that type of financial burden. They had already given up so much. The weight of their sacrifices pressed heavily on my shoulders, and though I longed for the future they dreamed of for me, the dream itself shimmered like something just out of reach, visible, beautiful, but always slipping through my fingers.

Then one Tuesday morning in my sophomore year of high school, when my mom was trying to get me out of bed for school, she told me a plane had crashed into a building. At first, I thought she was just trying to get me out of bed. But when I got out of bed, I realized she was serious. She was frozen in front of the television, her face pale and her eyes locked on the screen. That day, September 11, everything changed. Like the rest of the country, we were shocked and afraid, but for us, the fear ran far deeper. None of us knew what would come next for my brother in the Marines, but we all sensed that life had just changed forever.

In the subsequent months and years, those fears transformed into our reality. My brother was sent on multiple deployments to Iraq, Kuwait, and Afghanistan. Each trip was like a silent storm in our home, casting a shadow over every room and conversation. My parents watched the news every night, clinging to every word, their faces tense, their hands slightly trembling as they held the remote. Back then, there were no texts or quick updates. If he didn't call, the hours felt endless, each minute a stark reminder of what could go wrong at any time.

The phone became both our lifeline and our tormentor. Every time it rang, our bodies jolted with the same mix of hope and fear. One time in particular, the phone rang as we were getting ready for bed late in the evening, and I nearly tripped rushing to grab it.

"Hello?" I whispered, breathless.

"Hey, it's me," my brother's voice crackled through the line. Relief washed over me.

"How's school going?" he asked, his tone casual, as if we weren't separated by a war zone.

"It's okay," I said quickly. I was tired from school and the heaviness at home, but it felt small compared to what he faced overseas. "I'm keeping up."

Behind me, my mom's anxious voice urged, "¿Está bien? Pregúntale si está bien." My dad leaned forward, his eyes fixed on me, waiting for an answer.

"They want to know if you're okay," I said.

"I'm fine," he replied. "Tell them not to worry."

I passed the phone to my parents, watching as they relaxed at the sound of his voice. For a few minutes, the storm inside our home calmed down.

But when the call ended, the silence that followed always hit harder—the distance between him and us and the constant fear of imminent danger still tormented us. And so, the cycle repeated itself: the long stretches of waiting, the desperate jumps whenever the phone rang, the momentary relief, and then the heavy silence that settled in once more.

My parents leaned into their faith. They prayed throughout the day, lighting candles and whispering promises to La Virgen de Guadalupe. "Cuando regrese sano y salvo, vamos a ir todos a ver a la Virgencita en la Ciudad de México" they would both promise. If he came home safe, we would all go to the Basilica of Our Lady of Guadalupe and give thanks.

Despite the constant undercurrent of worry, we still had to go on with brushing our teeth every day, I had to study for science class, my dad had to build houses, my mom had to cook, we had to sing happy birthday to one another as our birthdays came and went, we watched *Sábado Gigante*. Even in the face of fear and uncertainty, life went on. We kept hoping. We kept believing. We found a way to keep going.

My brother came home from one of his deployments when I was in junior high school. As my parents promised in their thousands of prayers, we made a pilgrimage by bus as a family to La Basilica in Mexico City. The bus ride felt long, as always. When we arrived in Mexico City, we squeezed into a taxi and crawled through traffic, cars honking, people yelling out of their car at other drivers, vendors trying to sell us fruit at each red light. When we arrived at the Basilica, the taxi dropped us off at the end of the plaza facing the Basilica. It was full of people. Many of them pilgrims delivering on a promise like us. We passed by many vendors selling candles, rosaries and laminated prayer cards. Once we made it to the entrance, we stood there trying to take it all in. At the end of the altar stood La Virgen de Guadalupe.

When my dad reached the threshold, without saying a word, he lowered himself to the hard stone floor. Just as he had promised the Virgencita he would do if she brought his son home safely, he entered the Basilica crawling on his knees. Each slow and steady step showed the gratitude and faith he carried. When we all reached La Virgen, although this was not the end of my brother's military career, we were happy he was with us for the time being. He went on additional deployments, but he continued to come home safely after each one, and my parents are sure it was la Virgencita keeping her half of the celestial covenant.

Later that year, my uncle offered me my first job at his construction business where my dad and many of my uncles and cousins worked. I helped his secretary with filing documents, answering phones, and other basic administrative tasks. It was my first glimpse into an office environment, and I started daydreaming about a career with a business casual dress code and a name plate on my desk. Nobody in my family had a job like that. To me, achieving that dream meant I had made it, that I had reached stability, and that my parents' dreams for me had come true.

But those daydreams were always followed by a jolt of reality when I returned home and heard my parents say, "Que no hay dinero." There's no money. I had no idea how I was going to turn those dreams into reality when it felt like we were living paycheck to paycheck.

By the time I reached my senior year, I started missing school more and more often. Since we did not have the money for a four-year university, I could not see a path to college. I lost the motivation to keep my grades up or even try applying to schools. Because my parents were always working, they did not realize I was skipping classes.

One afternoon, instead of going to math class, I went home early. While waiting for my cup of noodles to cook, a bag of Hot Cheetos already torn open on the counter, I checked the mail and saw a letter from my high school. It was a truancy notice. My heart sank. I quickly tore it up and tossed it away. I didn't want my parents to see it or have to explain. I knew they'd be disappointed, and I didn't want to add another worry to their list.

Their minds were already somewhere else, thousands of miles away with my brother, wondering if he was safe and praying that he would make it home. Compared to that, my slipping grades and uncertain plans after high school felt invisible, like a problem too small to matter. Still, inside, I carried both guilt for not trying harder and relief that no one was pressing me for answers I did not have.

Although my grades began to slip, I still managed to graduate. Looking back now, I realize I could have done more to explore my options. I could have searched for scholarships, asked more questions, or leaned on my school counselors for guidance. But at the time, I didn't know what questions to ask or even where to begin. I even considered not going to college. We didn't have the money, and I had no idea what I wanted to study or which career path to choose, but I also didn't want to let my parents down. Their dream of me graduating from college became my own. I would close my eyes and visualize myself walking across the stage, hearing my name called, and feeling the pride in that moment as if it were already mine.

In the end, uncertainty didn't stop me from moving forward, it simply shaped the path I took next. After graduating from high school, I attended Evergreen Valley College since it was close to home and took general education courses while I figured out my next steps. I qualified for financial aid, easing the pressure of how we would pay for college. Around the same time, I started working at a women's clothing retail store in the mall. I enjoyed it because I would get an employee discount. I also opened my first bank account to deposit my checks. For the first time, I was responsible for covering my own expenses.

That marked the beginning of juggling work and school, a balancing act that would shape not only my college years but also my career and, in many ways, my identity as a first-gen student. What I didn't know then was that soon, I would land my first office job, a job that promised money and opportunity, but also introduced me to the weight of financial pressure in an entirely new way.

Chapter 4

New Beginnings

During my first semester at community college, I felt excited to start college and make my parents proud. However, I also felt uncertain about what to major in and what career path to choose. It was a fresh start with new things to learn and people to meet. I also felt intimidated by the new expectations and feeling like I was navigating this uncharted territory without a GPS to guide me.

I made a new friend in English class, and we shared what we did for work. He mentioned he worked in a mortgage office, and I mentioned that I was looking for work opportunities outside of retail. Then he said, "Do you want to work with me doing cold calling?"

"Cold calling?" I asked. It was my first time hearing the term.

He smiled and explained, "They give you a list of people who might want to refinance their homes, and you call them to see if they're interested. If you help close a deal, you can make a few thousand dollars."

Thousands of dollars?! He had my attention. Oh, what I could do with thousands of dollars! This was just the kind of professional job my parents had always hoped I'd have: an office setting, a desk, business attire.

My friend set me up with an interview with his two managers. I wore black pants with a button-up shirt. I was excited about the opportunity and nervous about what questions they would ask me during the interview. Surprisingly, the questions were simple. They asked me about my customer service experience and how I would handle an upset customer. They also asked if I spoke another language, I said yes, Spanish. They smiled and said, "That's great, you'll be able to connect with more clients." Then they said, "When can you start?" I happily said, "How's next week?" I accepted the position without bothering to ask basic questions like if benefits were included. Honestly, I didn't mind. I saw a chance to improve my skillset and earn more money, and that was enough.

That semester, I only took two classes. I went to class in the mornings, then I'd go to the mortgage office for a few hours, then I'd finish the day working at the mall. I also worked at the mall for a few hours on the weekends. The rest of the time I did homework, spent time with my parents and friends. I was constantly on the move, chasing a future I wasn't sure how to reach, determined to keep trying.

The office environment was loud and fast-paced. It was a big office with rows of desks and phones, like a scene from *The Wolf of Wall Street*. On a busy day, there was over thirty people making calls at the same time. I sat at a desk in the same row as other junior reps, including my friend, with headset on, script in hand, dialing number after number.

Most of the time, people didn't answer. When someone did, they were usually annoyed or confused; some hung up on me mid-sentence, others yelled to stop calling them. I learned to shrug it off and keep dialing. The calls were transactional; there was no real connection, just a sales pitch disguised as "helping families save money." The few clients who showed interest were handed off to senior brokers. My job was only to get them in the door. At the end of the day, I had to report how many calls I made and how many referrals were made to senior brokers. The expectation was that I had to send at least one referral per hour, to "Always Be Closing." This was a line from the movie *Boiler Room,* that I was told to watch. It's about a brokerage firm selling dubious stocks with high-pressure sales tactics.

After a few months, I helped close my first deal, and my commission was a $2,000 paycheck. I had never held that much money in my hands before. I was so excited, I couldn't wait to tell my mom. But first, I went to the bank to deposit the check. While I was there, they even offered me a credit card with a $1,000 limit. I took it. I thought I was rich.

I proudly taped my paycheck stub to my bedroom wall like a trophy. As soon as the check was cleared, I took my mom out to eat at Denny's, one of her favorite places. It might not seem glamorous, but to us, it felt special. Sitting across from her in the booth, I grinned.

"Mamá, guess what? My first paycheck was two thousand dollars."

Her eyes widened. "¿De veras? Ay, mija, that's more than I used to make in a whole month."

I nodded, trying not to burst with pride. "I wanted to celebrate with you. I'm paying for lunch."

She shook her head, smiling softly. "Gracias mijita, estoy orgullosa de ti." "Thank you, Honey, I'm proud of you."

If I could, I would have pinned my mother saying those words to me to my door right next to the paystub.

That weekend, I went out with friends, treated them to lunch and dinner, bought new clothes and perfume, but this time, I went to Macys. I was living the life I thought I had dreamed of, until I wasn't. Before I knew it, the money was gone, and my credit card was maxed out.

My parents never had credit cards. They paid for everything in cash. If they had a bank account, it was only to cash their checks. We never talked about budgeting, balancing a checkbook, or paying off a credit card bill on time. I was learning all of it on my own, just like they once did.

A few months later, I closed another deal and my commission was $3,000. But instead of paying off my credit card, I saved half and spent the rest. Looking back, I realize I was still seeing money the way my parents had always shown me, with a scarcity mindset, and I hadn't yet learned how to manage it responsibly. That cycle quickly started to wear on me. The instability of the pay began to feel more like a gamble than a reward. I hated going weeks, or sometimes months, without a big paycheck, not knowing when the next deal would come through. I was learning the hard way that earning money didn't automatically mean security, and that mindset, shaped by my upbringing, would take years to unlearn.

But it wasn't just the money. The work itself started to feel hollow. I didn't like convincing people to refinance their homes when I didn't fully understand the process myself. I wasn't passionate about sales. I had taken the job because it looked and sounded like success, like the version of professionalism I thought I was supposed to chase. But in practice, it left me feeling empty. There was no real purpose behind the work, no deeper connection to the values that mattered most to me.

The excitement I had felt at the start, the sense that I was stepping into opportunity and success, began to fade. Instead of growth, I found myself enduring long hours of repetitive tasks, making endless cold calls, and facing pressure to chase numbers that never seemed to be enough. It didn't fit me—not my values, not my personality, not the future I wanted to build. Soon, not even the paycheck felt worth it anymore.

I knew what I had to do, but at the time, voluntarily leaving a desk job felt like voluntarily letting my family down. I was back to the drawing board trying to decide what career path I wanted to take, confused again. Will I ever figure it out? What career should I choose?

Looking back now, I understand it differently. Leaving that

job was an important step in discovering what fulfillment truly means. It showed me that success involves more than just a paycheck or a title. It also requires alignment, purpose, and recognizing your own worth. That experience became a valuable lesson in self-awareness, resilience, and having the courage to follow a path that felt authentic to my values. The disillusionment I experienced then wasn't a setback but a signal to push myself toward opportunities that matched who I was and who I aspired to be.

Around this time, my brother was stationed at Camp Pendleton, which brought a sense of relief to all of us. It meant we could see him more often, and my parents felt more at ease knowing he was close to home. Not long after, he got married and soon he and his new wife were expecting their first child. My parents were overjoyed about becoming grandparents, it was something they were looking forward to.

Many weekends, my mom, dad, and I would take a road trip down to Oceanside to visit him, driving eight hours on Friday night and coming back on Sunday. It became something we all looked forward to. I immediately fell in love with the area—the ocean breeze, the slower pace, the warmth of it all. I started looking into colleges in the area and daydreaming about transferring to San Diego State University. A new chapter began forming in my mind, and I felt ready for it.

I had just turned twenty, and I was ready to leave my parents' house and pursue something bigger. My hope was to transfer to a university in the San Diego area and begin building the life I had always dreamed about, but I couldn't do it alone.

I called my brother.

"Hey… can I ask you something?"

"Yeah, what's up?" he said casually.

"I've been thinking about moving out. I want to figure out my next steps, and I was wondering if I could stay with you for a while. Just until I get settled." A nervous smile tugged at my lips. "I want to transfer to a university in San Diego. I don't know, exactly how but I'll figure it out."

He was quiet for a moment, "Alright, sis. You can crash at my place. Just don't eat all my food."

I laughed in relief. "Deal."

As soon as I arrived in Oceanside, I began searching for both a job and a school. For a moment, I considered not continuing college at all. I still wasn't sure what I wanted to major in, and the idea of earning money right away felt tempting. But I kept hearing my parents' voices in my head, repeating the same lessons I had grown up with about the importance of a college education. I could also see it clearly in my mind: myself walking across the stage, hearing my name called, and feeling the pride and relief of making their dream, and now my dream, come true.

I found a nearby community college, Palomar College,

and enrolled online, signing up for two general education classes. It felt like a small step forward, even if I still didn't know exactly where I was headed. With only two classes per semester, graduation seemed like a distant dream, a milestone that felt far off but somehow worth working toward.

At the same time, I thought constantly about the kind of job I wanted, something professional, something that would allow me to dress up, walk into an office, and feel accomplished.

I applied to a few banks in the area. Luckily, I got an interview for a branch that was fifteen minutes away from my brother's house. I went to the in-person interview in black pants and a white button-down shirt. The service manager interviewed me and asked me a few questions about my customer service experience and if I had cash-handling experience. A few days later, I received a call from the service manager to offer me a part-time position. I was thrilled. It felt like I was one step closer to that version of myself I had always imagined: confident, capable, and finally stable. This was another opportunity to start again, and I was determined to make the most of it.

A few months after I moved to Oceanside, I received a call from my mom.

"Hi, Mija"

"Hi, Mami."

"I just wanted to tell you that I'm getting on the Greyhound tonight. I'll arrive in the morning."

"What? Tonight? By yourself?"

"Yes, by myself. It's fine. It's overnight. I'll sleep on the bus."

"Ok, I'll see you in the morning."

But the next morning, when I picked her up from the bus stop, I was surprised to see she had brought four suitcases with her.

"Mami... why do you have so many bags? How long are you planning to stay?" I asked, eyeing the suitcases.

She looked at me calmly, without hesitation. "Mija, I left your dad. I'm planning to live in Oceanside too."

"Wait... what? Really?"

She nodded. "Sí. It's time, and I want to be closer to you and your brother."

I sat there stunned, my heart racing. "I...I didn't expect this. But... if this is what you want, I'll help you."

Her face softened with relief. "Gracias, mija."

It caught me off guard, but I wasn't entirely surprised. My parents' relationship had never seemed like a loving one, at least not from what I had seen. They had stayed together for the sake of their children, and now that their job of raising us was mostly done, they were choosing different paths. I had never witnessed romantic, healthy love between them; it was just two adults trying to do their best to raise a family.

A part of me was relieved. I knew they weren't happy, and I was glad my mom was making the best choice for herself. I was also pleased that she was now closer to my brother and me. Her decision marked another shift in our family dynamic, one that, deep down, made sense. At the same time, moving out changed my relationship with my dad. We kept in touch, but we weren't as close as we had been, and the distance only grew once my mom, my brother, and I were living far away from him. I still respected him, still loved him, but our connection had shifted.

Honestly, I had secretly hoped this day would come ever since I found her crying in the bathroom. That moment never left me. I know my parents did their best to provide for us, and I'm forever grateful for their sacrifices, but I also saw the weight my mother carried every single day. She did everything in our home: all the cooking, cleaning, laundry, and taking care of us kids, while still holding a full-time job. She was always tired, always running on empty, yet she always managed to make it work.

It wasn't just her. I watched all my tías live the same story: overworked, overlooked, and often unappreciated. Deep down, I knew that wasn't the life I wanted for myself. So when my mom looked me in the eyes one day and said, "No termines como yo," I knew exactly what she meant.

She wasn't putting herself down, she was giving me a warning wrapped in love. She was urging me to dream bigger, to break cycles, to choose differently. And in that moment, I silently promised her and myself that I would. I didn't know how yet, but I was determined to build a life that would make her proud.

Nothing could have prepared me for what was going to happen in the next year with my mom, though. Just when I thought life was starting to settle into a new rhythm, everything shifted again. What came next would challenge me in ways I never saw coming.

Chapter 5

Navigating Challenges

My mom and I started looking for a place to live and luckily found a one-bedroom apartment in the same complex as my brother. The rent was $850 per month. It felt like a small win; being close to family during this transitional phase gave us both comfort. We were only a few doors away. The apartment was simple and almost empty when we moved in. We had little, just a couple of folding chairs and a basic bed we put together from Ikea that we shared. Our TV sat on a stack of cardboard boxes filled with old photo albums and family pictures, reminding us of our roots and past struggles. In the kitchen, we had a few mismatched utensils, plates, and mugs from the nearby dollar store. It wasn't fancy or fully furnished, but it was ours and full of hope. This modest, humble space soon became our sanctuary, a fresh start built with love and resilience.

My mom began searching for work, determined to help rebuild our lives. However, at the same time, I noticed something was changing in her health. When I was ten years old, she was diagnosed with type 2 diabetes. At the time, I didn't understand what that meant. All I knew was that my mom often complained of feeling tired, had trouble managing her weight, and mentioned going to the doctor or needing to take medication.

Looking back, her diagnosis was part of a much bigger issue. In the United States, more than 1 in 10 people have diabetes, and type 2 diabetes accounts for the vast majority of those cases. What's even more alarming is that Hispanic and Latino communities, like mine, are disproportionately affected. According to the CDC, Hispanic and Latino adults are more likely to develop diabetes than non-Hispanic white adults, and they often face more barriers to proper care and treatment. Diabetes isn't just an individual struggle, it's a community one, shaped by cultural, economic, and systemic challenges.

For my mom, those statistics weren't just numbers, they were her lived experience.

Over the years, I watched her health fluctuate. She would try to eat healthier, go on walks, and lose some weight, but it was always temporary. The weight would come back, and so would the exhaustion. The truth was, my mom was always taking care of everyone else, working, cooking, worrying, and leaving little energy for herself. She had grown up believing that sacrificing for your family was just what you did. But little by little, that sacrifice began to take a toll.

Her health decline didn't happen all at once, but it was steady and visible. She started to slow down going up the stairs. It was hard to watch someone so strong and selfless begin to struggle with the consequences of a disease that so many in our community live with. Diabetes became more than a diagnosis, it was a shadow that began to shape our daily lives.

She slowly began to notice swelling in her legs. At first, we thought it might be something minor, maybe she had been standing too long or eating something salty. But the swelling wouldn't go away. Concerned, we went to the doctor. As always, I sat beside her during the appointment, serving as her interpreter like I had been doing for years, even though I was still learning how to navigate it all myself.

The doctor suspected she had a heart condition that was affecting her circulation, which would explain the swelling, so he referred her to a cardiologist for further testing. Soon after, the cardiologist started her on blood pressure medication and began closely monitoring her heart by having regular appointments. He also recommended that she begin a strict, low-sodium diet to help manage her symptoms. We hoped these changes would help reduce the swelling and offer some relief, but they didn't. Some days were better than others, but the swelling persisted.

At home, I did everything I could to support her. I began cooking low-sodium meals, carefully reading food labels, limiting processed foods, and experimenting with herbs and spices to make things taste better. I ate the same meals she did, not just out of convenience, but out of solidarity. I didn't want her to feel like she was doing it alone. We were in this together.

Despite our efforts, the swelling didn't fully go away. Some days, the discomfort was so bad it hurt her to walk. We kept her legs elevated, hoping it would ease the pain. But it was hard to watch her suffer and feel like nothing we were doing was enough.

We kept going back and forth to doctors' offices, trying to find answers. They increased her dosage and tried new prescriptions, but nothing really made a difference. Every appointment felt like one step forward and two steps back. It was frustrating and disheartening, and I could see the toll it was taking on her, not just physically but emotionally as well.

At just 21, I was barely holding myself together. I was taking a few general education classes but couldn't concentrate. I'd sit in the back, staring at the board while my mind drifted back home to my mom. I kept thinking,"What if something happens while I'm not there? What if I'm not doing enough?" I didn't know what I wanted for my future and didn't have the mental or emotional strength to find out. I was just surviving, constantly anxious. My chest was always tight, like I was bracing for the worst, waiting for bad news. I carried the heavy responsibility to be my mom's advocate and caregiver, to speak for her when she couldn't, but I was only pretending to be strong. I would sit by hospital walls, nodding through baffling conversations with doctors—heart pounding, palms sweating—afraid to ask the wrong questions. Most nights, I cried quietly in the dark, overwhelmed and burdened. I was scared, exhausted, and more than anything, painfully alone.

My brother, who might've been the one person I could

lean on, was deployed again, and I didn't feel like I could reach out to my dad for help. This was about my mom, and she had made it clear she wanted nothing to do with him. So I kept everything in. I didn't ask for help. I didn't want to worry anyone. But inside, I felt like I had the weight of the world on my shoulders. I was doing my best to take her to appointments and remain positive, but I also couldn't help but think, "What if she doesn't get better?"

To cope with everything unraveling at home, I started going out with friends on the weekends, drinking, dancing, pretending I was someone else for a few hours. I just wanted to feel free, to laugh without guilt, to forget how heavy everything felt. But even in the middle of the noise and music, I couldn't silence the ache in my chest.

One time while standing in a crowded bar, vodka cranberry drink in hand, watching my friends talk about classes and weekend trips like it was the most natural thing in the world, I felt so envious that their biggest worries were midterms or who liked who, nothing like the worries waiting for me at home. I wasn't bitter, I didn't want their lives. I just wanted a version of mine that didn't revolve around hospitals, medications, or monitoring my mom's swollen legs. I wanted to be able to care about school the way they did, without my thoughts constantly drifting to whether or not my mom was okay.

I smiled and took another sip of my drink, trying to drown the guilt that came with wanting more than the life I was leading. Partying became my escape, a few blurry hours when I could pretend I wasn't carrying so much. But the moment the night ended, and I was back in my room, the weight returned. Heavier. Always heavier.

And what happens after a night of drinking? Hangovers. And with them came a wave of guilt and emotional exhaustion. The very problems I had tried to forget the night before were still there, waiting for me in the morning. Nothing had changed.

My mom would gently tell me that I shouldn't be drinking, but her concern only made me feel more irritated.

"Mija," she said softly one evening, "Ya no tomes tanto. It's not good for you."

I sighed, looking away. "Mami, I'm fine. It helps me relax, that's all."

Her eyes lingered on me, full of worry. "I just don't want to see you hurt yourself."

Her words pierced deeper than I wanted to admit. I didn't want another reminder of what I already knew: I was spiraling. I thought about going to therapy, but the idea of adding one more appointment to my already packed schedule felt impossible. I was already juggling her medical visits, work, my classes, and my emotions.

Desperate for something, anything, that might help me cope, I turned to the internet and stumbled across an article about meditation. I had heard of it before, but no one in my family practiced it. It felt unfamiliar, even a little strange, but I figured it was worth a try. One day, I sat down cross-legged on the living room floor, just like I had seen in pictures of monks. I closed my eyes and set a timer for five minutes.

Almost immediately, my mind took off. Instead of silence, there was noise. Thoughts I didn't even know I was carrying started to race: my mom's next doctor's appointment, the unread chapters for class, the pile of dishes in the sink, my unpaid bills. I had assumed meditation would bring peace, but instead, it felt like my mind was mocking me. After a few failed attempts, I gave up and told myself maybe this just wasn't for me. Maybe my mind was too loud, too anxious, too much. Maybe this was something I had to learn to live with.

But I didn't forget about it.

Months later, a guest on a podcast mentioned that meditation wasn't about silencing your thoughts, it was about observing them, like watching clouds go by. That simple shift in perspective cracked something open in me. I had been approaching meditation with the idea that I had to be still, quiet, perfect. But maybe the practice wasn't about controlling the chaos, it was about learning to sit with it.

So I tried again. This time, I let the thoughts come. I didn't judge them or try to push them away. I just noticed them, like clouds. Slowly, five minutes turned into ten. The practice didn't fix everything overnight, but it gave me moments of calm in the middle of the storm. And eventually, those moments became something I could return to, my own small way of finding peace.

Chapter 6

A New Normal

My mom's legs continued to get worse. I could see the pain on her face even when she tried to hide it. One night, she told me she wasn't feeling well. I asked if she wanted me to take her to the emergency room, but she said no. Hoping she'd start to feel better with some rest, she told me to wait until the morning. Around 5 a.m., she woke me up frightened, her voice weak.

"Ya no puedo más… no puedo respirar," she whispered.

"Mamá, what's wrong?!" I shot up from bed, my heart racing.

"I can't take it anymore, I can't breathe," she repeated, her face pale.

"Okay, okay," I said, fumbling for my clothes with shaking hands. "I'll take you to the hospital right now."

I tore clothes out of my drawer, not caring what was going where, just that I was clothed at all. I grabbed my keys, and helped her down the stairs to the car, my mind thinking of every negative outcome as she sat in the front seat, head against the cool passenger window while I rushed her to the emergency room. When we arrived at the passenger drop off, I ran inside to see if I could get a wheelchair and a nurse to help. Luckily, there was one waiting. The nurse brought the wheelchair outside as I helped her get out of the car and into the wheelchair. Then he wheeled her in while I went to find a parking spot.

Since she was struggling to breathe, they took her in right away, and I followed behind. The small hospital room felt suffocating as the nurses and techs rushed around, their voices overlapping, and the machines beeping. They moved fast, hooking her up to monitors, checking her vitals, asking question after question that I tried to translate. I stood in the corner trying to take deep breaths. But inside, a wave of fear and anxiety rolled over me. My mind raced with all the things that could go wrong, each thought darker than the last. What if it's a heart attack? How long will she stay here? What if she doesn't recover? I was terrified I might lose her, that the person who had been my anchor through everything might suddenly not be there anymore.

A couple of hours passed and things began to settle. As nurses continued running tests, I stepped outside to call the bank where I was working. My hands were trembling as I dialed, my mind already racing ahead. How long would we be here? How serious was this going to be? Still, I figured this was going to be a quick call. Just a heads-up.

"Hey," I said when my boss picked up the phone. "I'm at the hospital with my mom. I won't be coming in today."

There was a pause. Then she said it, so casually, as if I had just mentioned I was running late for coffee.

"Well, we have a meeting this morning at ten. Can you come in for that?"

I was confused. For a second, I thought I misheard her. My brain couldn't process it fast enough. "What?" My jaw tightened, my stomach churned. A flood of thoughts rushed in at once. Is she serious? How can she even ask me that? Does she not hear the fear in my voice?

I was standing in the hallway watching my mom in a hospital bed breathing from a tube and wires coming out of her chest, and now I had to explain why I wasn't available for a meeting?

Anger flooded my body.

"My mom is in the hospital," I said, louder this time. "I'm not coming in." I didn't wait for a response. I hung up.

For a few seconds, I just stood there, staring at the phone screen, my heart pounding. A wave of guilt mixed with rage hit me. Do I need to worry about losing my job on top of everything else?

I took deep breaths and forced myself to refocus. I couldn't let that take over. Not now. My mom needed me. She was all that mattered.

I went back into the hospital room, sat beside her, and

held her hand. I didn't know what news we'd get or what the next few days would look like, but at that moment, all I knew was that I needed to be there for her.

Later that afternoon, the doctors finally gave me some answers. The reason my mom had been struggling to breathe was because her lungs were filled with fluid. Hearing that made my heart sink, but at least we knew why she couldn't breathe. They started her on Lasix, a medication used to remove excess fluid from the body. The goal was to relieve the pressure on her lungs so she could breathe more easily.

Once she was stable, they admitted her to the main hospital and moved her out of the emergency room and into a different room. We started to settle in, knowing this wasn't going to be a quick visit. The doctors said it would likely take a few days before she could go home. I stayed by her side all day, every day, holding her hand, helping her with anything she needed, and doing my best to keep her spirits up. When visitor hours ended in the evening, I would reluctantly go home, only to return early the next morning. I didn't want her to feel alone, not even for a moment.

I sat by her bedside, watching closely as the medication began to work. Slowly, her body began releasing the fluid. I could hear a difference in her breathing; it was still difficult but improving. They placed an oxygen mask on her to help her breathe more comfortably, and I could see her body begin to relax.

It became a waiting game. Doctors and nurses rotated in and out of the room throughout the day, each one checking her vitals, adjusting medications, and asking questions. One of them was a cardiologist who explained they were keeping a close eye on her heart. I braced myself every time a new doctor walked in, afraid they might bring more bad news.

Thankfully, the doctor's confirmed it wasn't a heart attack. That brought a huge sense of relief to myself and my mom. However, we still didn't know the cause. After a few days in the hospital, a new doctor, a nephrologist, came in to check on my mom. At the time, I didn't know what that meant. He introduced himself and explained, "I'm a kidney specialist."

He reviewed her chart, looked up at me, and asked, "When was your mom diagnosed with kidney failure?"

Kidney failure? I blinked, unsure if I'd heard him right.

"Kidney failure?" I repeated, confused and panicked. "I don't know anything about that. No one has ever told us she had any problems with her kidneys."

I stared at him, waiting for his face to show some sign that this was a mistake. Maybe he was looking at the wrong chart. Maybe this was just a miscommunication. But he nodded slowly, his expression serious, as if he already knew the weight of what he was about to say.

"That's likely why her legs have been swelling," he

explained. "It's not just poor circulation, it's because her kidneys are losing function and not removing excess fluid from her body."

My heart sank. My hands went cold. I sat frozen, trying to make sense of what I was hearing. Kidney failure. Not poor circulation. Not heart issues. This was the first time anyone had said those words to us.

A flurry of thoughts flooded my mind: How did no one catch this? How long has this been going on? What does this mean for her? For us?

A surge of anger rose up in my throat, directed at every doctor we'd seen before. How could something this serious have been missed? How could we have gone so long trusting what turned out to be incomplete answers?

I looked over at my mom, who was resting, unaware of the conversation unfolding outside the curtain. She had been carrying this with her for so long, trusting, believing. And now, it felt like we were only beginning to uncover the real story, piece by piece.

At the time, I didn't know that 1 in 7 adults in the U.S. has chronic kidney disease, according to the National Institute on Diabetes and Digestive and Kidney Diseases. That's nearly 37 million people, and many don't even know they have it. I also learned that it affects about 14% of Hispanic adults, and that the leading causes of kidney failure are diabetes and high blood pressure, both of which my mom had been living with for years.

Knowing this, I couldn't help but wonder if we had been told earlier, could something have been done to slow it down? Could this have been prevented or managed differently?

This new information changed everything. It reframed how we saw her health and added another layer to the care and support she would need moving forward. And for me, it was a painful reminder of how easily things can be overlooked. Were there questions I could have asked that I didn't? Did I not advocate for my mom well enough? I blamed myself.

After I had a day to process the news about her kidneys, the shock began to wear off, and I shifted into action mode. I started asking more questions. "How is kidney failure going to be treated? Does she need to change her medication? Does her diet need to change?" I wanted to understand what this meant for her daily life, for her future. I was ready to hear the plan, prepared to adjust and support her in whatever came next.

But then came more news, even more unexpected. The nephrologist sat me down, his expression calm but serious. "Based on her lab results," he said, "she will most likely need dialysis treatment."

Dialysis. I'd heard of it before, vaguely, but it had always belonged to someone else's story, not mine. Not hers.

"What is that?" I asked, trying to remain calm, but a tightening sensation grew in my chest.

He explained that when the kidneys lose almost all their function, dialysis becomes the only solution. A machine would then need to perform the work her body can no longer do, filtering waste, toxins, and excess fluid from her blood. She would have to go to a dialysis clinic three times a week, with each session lasting three to four hours.

I felt myself shrinking in that chair. "For how long?" I asked, hoping that this was a temporary treatment.

He paused, his voice soft, but it still struck me.

"For the rest of her life... unless she receives a kidney transplant."

The rest of her life? My scattered thoughts of what that truly meant paralyzed me. I had walked into that day hoping for clarity, maybe a new medication, a care plan, something manageable. I wasn't ready for this. I wasn't ready to hear that my mom's life would now revolve around machines and appointments... or that her only alternative was something as rare and uncertain as a transplant.

The reality hit me gradually, starting with disbelief and turning into dread. I glanced at my mom, trying to grasp the impact of what we had just been told. Her entire life was about to shift, and ours as well. I was only 21 trying to figure out my own life. I grieved that that "normal" life I wanted to lead was never going to be mine now. How was I going to get her to her treatments while also going to school and work so I could pay our bills? Should I drop out of school? How is this going to work? How was I going to find a way forward? And yet, in the midst of the fear and uncertainty, I clung to one clear vision: myself walking across the graduation stage, hearing my name called, and proving to myself, and to my parents, that I could find a way forward no matter what.

Fortunately, the doctor knew some Spanish. He carefully explained everything to my mom, and I just watched as she took in the information. I was too overwhelmed to speak and focused on staying strong for her. My mind was spinning as I tried to understand what this would mean for us. I didn't want to cry or frighten her; I simply listened.

To my surprise, she stayed calm. There was no fear in her eyes, no anger in her voice. My mom had always been a woman of strong faith, and after the doctor finished explaining, she simply nodded and said, "Si eso es lo que Dios quiere, está bien." If this is what God wants for me, then it's okay.

I felt my chest tighten. "Mami, I don't know how we're going to do this," I whispered, my voice breaking. "Dialysis, the schedule, your health… it feels like too much."

She reached for my hand. "Todo va a estar bien, mija. Dios aprieta pero no ahorca. We'll figure this out, like we always do."

Tears blurred my vision. "But I don't want to see you experience this."

Her gaze softened. "I understand. We will handle it day

by day. Don't stress too much. You're stronger than you believe, and I am too."

Her calmness strengthened me. Although my heart was heavy for all she was about to go through, I believed we would handle it together. This was our new reality, and in some way, we would navigate it one dialysis session and one day at a time.

It had been nearly a week since my mom was hospitalized. We had been stuck in a routine of uncertainty monitoring her vital signs, awaiting test results, and coming to terms with her diagnosis. When the doctors finally discussed discharging her, I felt a tentative wave of relief but soon it was overshadowed by a knot of anxiety in my chest. Going home didn't mean life returned to normal; it signified that the real work was just starting.

A social worker spoke to us before her discharge, reviewing my mom's diagnosis and explaining what to expect next. She clarified that kidney failure was now a part of her life, as well as ours. The only relief was that my mom now qualified for Medicare, so we wouldn't have to worry about treatment costs. She gave us papers with her weekly dialysis schedule and confirmed her first appointment at the clinic, which was set for 6 a.m.

Waking up for an appointment at 6 a.m. three times a week meant dealing with early mornings, long days, and juggling drop-offs and pick-ups around work, school, grocery shopping, and doing laundry. The burden felt heavy, but I didn't face it alone. I contacted my brother, luckily he wasn't on deployment at the time.

"It's going to be a lot, and I can't do it all by myself. Can you help me figure this out?"

"Of course," he said without hesitation. "Tell me the schedule. What days are we talking about?"

"Three times a week, at six in the morning," I explained, exhaustion already creeping into my voice. "That means drop-offs, pick-ups, and making sure everything lines up with work and school."

He let out a low whistle. "That's rough. But we'll split it. I can take Mondays and Wednesdays. Can you handle Fridays?"

"Yeah, I can do Fridays. Thank you... seriously. I was scared I'd have to figure this all out alone."

"You're not alone," he said firmly. "We'll make it work."

On days when I had work or class, my sister-in-law would step in. In the afternoons, depending on who was available, one of us would pick her up. It was a careful balancing act, but we were dedicated to making it work. We all helped out, doing our best to support her and each other as we adjusted to our new normal.

It wasn't easy. The emotional toll of seeing her so dependent on a machine, the physical exhaustion from constant coordination, and the fears that crept in between moments, it was a lot. During that time, I often questioned whether I could keep up with school. Some days, the thought of dropping out felt like the only way to make everything more manageable. But this was our family. And when one of us needed help, we showed up. No matter how tired we were, no matter how uncertain the path ahead seemed, we were in it together.

Chapter 7

Focusing on the Dream

As we all adjusted to our new normal, I slowly shifted my focus back to school. Life still felt uncertain, but I knew that continuing my education was one of the few things I could control. That semester, I enrolled in a public speaking class. At first, the thought of standing in front of people made my stomach twist into knots, but something about it sparked my curiosity. It was the first time I felt a genuine interest in a subject, even if it scared me.

To my surprise, I did well, turning in my assignments on time, earning good grades on my presentations, and continuing that success in my subsequent communications courses. I realized I had a natural ability to connect ideas, to express myself, and to listen—skills I had unknowingly sharpened while advocating for my mom and navigating her many doctor's appointments. That's when it clicked: I would major in communications. It felt like the right fit: broad enough to open doors in multiple fields, yet meaningful enough to feel like a purpose.

I made an appointment with my academic advisor, and during our meeting, they informed me that I was nearing the number of credits required to transfer to a university. I was getting closer to achieving both my dream and my parents' dreams. I had always dreamed of attending San Diego State University, but it was a one-hour drive with no traffic. I knew I needed to stay closer to home. The university closest to home was California State University, San Marcos, a fifteen-minute drive, so I applied there. It wasn't my original plan, but it felt like the right decision for that season of life. My dreams were still intact; they were just taking a different route.

At home, dialysis took a toll on my mom physically and emotionally. There were many days she seemed utterly drained, her face filled with fatigue and spending most of the day in bed. It was heartbreaking to watch her struggle through the fatigue, nausea, and pain that sometimes followed her treatments.

During one of her follow-up visits, her nephrologist shared some encouraging news: He believed my mom might be a candidate for a kidney transplant. It wasn't the first time the topic had come up. In a previous conversation, he had asked if anyone in our family would be willing to donate a kidney. Without hesitation, my mom said no. She was firm in her decision. She didn't want my brother or me to even consider it. "You might need it one day," she had told us. Her protectiveness never wavered, even when she was the one in need.

The nephrologist referred her to UC San Diego for a full evaluation. This marked the beginning of a new chapter; several months filled with appointments. There were consultations with cardiologists to test the strength of her heart, endocrinologists to evaluate how her body managed diabetes, social workers to assess her support system, and transplant coordinators who explained the long list of protocols we would need to follow.

Some appointments required her to be hooked up to monitors, while others involved repeated blood draws to evaluate her organ function and compatibility markers. We filled out countless questionnaires about mental health, daily habits, and lifestyle. We answered question after question: Who would care for her after surgery? Could she manage dozens of medications? Did she have reliable transportation to attend every follow-up appointment? Did she fully understand the risks?

The evaluation process also required us to attend classes designed to prepare patients and families for life before and after transplant. We sat through sessions that explained the transplant process step by step, nutritional classes that taught us how her diet would need to change, and medication workshops outlining the strict regimen she would have to follow for the rest of her life.

At every visit, they were trying to determine whether my mom would be a reliable transplant recipient. They needed to be sure she could care for herself, had a strong support system, could follow a strict medication regimen, and would keep up with the demanding post-surgery protocols.

One major requirement stood out: if she were approved

and received a transplant, she would need a caregiver by her side 24/7 during the critical recovery period the first few months after the transplant. That responsibility would, of course, fall on me.

I knew it wouldn't be easy. Caregiving meant more than simply being present, it meant becoming her scheduler, chauffeur, medication manager, and emotional anchor all at once. I would need to track a long list of medications taken at exact hours of the day and night, monitor her for signs of infection or organ rejection, take and record vital signs, and make sure she followed strict dietary restrictions. I would also have to learn how to give her insulin injections, something she hadn't needed before. The first month, I would have to take her to UCSD Medical Center, a fifty-minute drive, three times a week for blood work and follow-up appointments, which meant early mornings since my mom had to be fasting for the bloodwork.

It meant putting my life on pause. I would need to take family leave from work, make arrangements with my professors so I wouldn't fall behind in my classes, and rebuild my daily routine around her healing. But I didn't hesitate. My mom had given me everything she could growing up. Now, it was my turn to be there for her in every way I could.

We made it to all of her appointments and completed the required classes. Some days were exhausting, but we kept showing up anyway. Even after we checked the last box on the to-do list, there was no guarantee that she would be placed on the transplant list. Months went by. I finished a semester of school and I kept taking my mom to dialysis. Then finally, my mom received a letter from UCSD giving her the incredible news that she would be placed on the transplant list to receive a kidney. I called my brother to give him the good news. We were happy and grateful for this opportunity. Although we knew the wait could be anywhere from five to ten years, just knowing she was on the list filled us with hope. It meant there was a chance. It meant we could still believe in a better outcome.

Trying to juggle everything was incredibly frustrating at times. Between caring for my mom, working, and attending school part-time, I often felt stretched thin. There were moments, more than I like to admit, when I questioned whether I should keep attending classes. Should I drop out of school? Was it worth it? Would I ever finish at this pace? It felt like I was moving in slow motion while the rest of the world sped by. I watched my classmates register for full course loads and talk about transferring or graduating, while I was doing everything I could just to make it through one or two classes at a time. I constantly felt like I was behind, like I wasn't doing enough, no matter how hard I tried. I compared myself to others and felt stuck, as if everyone else were sprinting ahead while I tried to stay afloat.

But through all the doubt, one image kept me going, the dream of walking across a graduation stage, cap and gown on, seeing my parents' faces in the crowd. That vision carried me through some of my lowest days.

Then one afternoon, everything changed. I received a letter

in the mail from California State University San Marcos. I carried the letter inside, placed it on the kitchen counter dreading opening it. I showed my mom the envelope, and she said, "Open it!" in Spanish. As I opened it, my heart raced, hoping for the best but bracing for disappointment. My mom was in my ear, "What does it say? Did you get in?" There it was, in bold letters- **Congratulations on your acceptance.**

I stared at the words for a few seconds in disbelief, and then the tears came. I cried with happiness, relief, and overwhelming pride. I did it. After everything, every long night studying, the stress of taking care of my mom, every moment I thought about dropping out of school, I was finally taking the next big step. I hugged my mom and told her I was accepted. She was happy and proud that I was getting closer to achieving not just my dream, but the dream they had carried for me since the beginning.

All of their sacrifices, the long hours, the unseen struggles, were finally bearing fruit. This moment felt like it belonged to all of us. With each step I took, I was getting closer to realizing the vision I had held onto for so long: walking across the graduation stage and hearing my name called.

The summer before starting at the university was filled with excitement and anticipation. I was finally going to attend a university, a dream I had carried with me for years. It felt like everything was finally aligning, and for once, I allowed myself to feel proud. I moved in with roommates and my mom moved in with my brother since he recently bought a house and had more space. However, they now lived forty-five minutes away.

When it was time to register for classes, I eagerly logged into the student portal. I browsed through the course catalog, selected my classes, and felt a rush of energy. I was doing it, I was really going to be a university student. But that excitement quickly faded the moment I reached the checkout screen. My heart dropped. I had never seen a balance so high in my life.

Panic set in. I tried to calm my nerves and immediately submitted my financial aid application, holding on to the hope that it would cover the costs like it had before. But a few days later, the response hit me like a brick wall: I no longer qualified. How could I not qualify anymore? Did I do something wrong? How am I supposed to pay for school now?

The year before, I had accepted a promotion at the bank where I worked. It was a much-needed raise, and I had been proud of that step forward. I went from making $12.50 per hour to $17 per hour. I needed the money to cover my expenses and save some money, so of course I said yes. What I didn't realize at the time was how that raise would impact my financial aid eligibility. On paper, it looked like I made too much. But in reality, it still wasn't nearly enough to cover tuition, fees, and textbooks, not to mention living expenses.

I felt stuck with nowhere to turn. I couldn't ask my parents for help; they simply didn't have the means. Fear began to settle in. Had I made it this far just to give up because

I couldn't afford it? I cried the entire day, overwhelmed by desperation and disappointment. It felt unfair. I had worked so hard, sacrificed so much, and now money stood in the way. I felt like I couldn't catch a break.

But the next day, I dried my tears and looked for solutions. I wasn't ready to let go of my dream. I researched options on the university website, and I learned I could apply for student loans through the website. The idea terrified me. Taking on debt felt like such a heavy burden. How would I pay this off later? What if I never could? My mind spiraled with questions, but deep down, I knew this was the only way forward.

With trembling hands and a racing heart, I stared at the numbers on the screen. I was approved for a student loan in the thousands to cover my tuition costs. I was hesitant to click accept. It wasn't ideal, but it was my only option forward. I told myself I'd figure out how to pay them off later. Right now, I just needed to take the next step. And that's precisely what I did.

My first day at Cal State San Marcos was filled with excitement and a deep sense of accomplishment. I felt like I had finally made it. As I walked across the campus, I was in awe; it felt massive compared to the community college campuses I had attended before. The buildings, the buzz of students, and the energy of the university environment made it all feel real. I was officially a university student.

Thanks to the student loans I had accepted, I was able to cover my tuition, buy a parking pass, and purchase the textbooks I needed. I also made a big decision to switch work locations. I transferred to a bank that was open on weekends, so I could create a more flexible schedule and prioritize my classes during the week. Every choice I made was intentional, focused on one goal: graduating within two years.

To make that happen, I pushed myself beyond what I was used to. I enrolled in more than the usual two classes, knowing that if I stayed longer than two years, the cost would pile up. I didn't want to take on any more debt than I already had. The course load was intense; I was a full-time student taking four courses a semester. Three of my classes were in the morning, then I'd head to the bank to work for a few hours, then back to school for an evening class. I'd work every Saturday and Sunday at the bank and used the evenings to complete my assignments and study. Juggling everything wasn't easy, but I kept telling myself this was temporary. I reminded myself every day: This is a season of sacrifice. If I stay focused, I'll get through it. And when the days felt especially heavy, I returned to the vision that had carried me this far: the image of me walking across the graduation stage, in a cap and gown, with my family watching proudly from the crowd. That dream kept me grounded and gave me the strength to keep pushing forward.

That semester when I no longer qualified for financial aid, something shifted in me. I thought success was linear, that if I worked hard, stayed focused, and followed the right steps, everything would fall into place. But seeing the cost of college taught me that success isn't just about effort, it's also about navigating setbacks, making tough decisions, and pushing through fear. Accepting student loans wasn't easy, but it reminded me that sometimes the path forward isn't perfect—just possible. Before this, I thought perseverance meant working harder and never giving up. Now, I began to understand that perseverance means doing what you can with what you have, even when it scares you. From that semester on, I carried a new mindset: I may not have all the answers or resources, but I'll always find a way. And that was enough to keep me going.

Chapter 8

A Second Chance

I was genuinely enjoying my time at the university. Despite the increased class load and heavier workload, life didn't feel so heavy. For the first time in a long while, I felt like I could breathe. I was meeting new people in class, formed friendships, and immersed myself in classes that actually sparked my interest. I felt like I belonged, like I was finally stepping into the version of myself I had worked so hard to become.

One of the best opportunities I came across was a mentorship program offered by the university. I first spotted a colorful flyer pinned to a bulletin board on campus, its bold letters promising guidance and growth, with a website to sign up. I hesitated for a moment, unsure what to expect, but something nudged me forward. I signed up, hopeful that this program might help me find the direction and support I had been looking for.

To my surprise and luck, I was matched with a mentor who changed my sense of what was possible. She became my mentor throughout my time at the university. A professor of communications, she was the first Latina I had ever met in my field with a Ph.D. I was in awe of someone who looked like me, who came from a similar background, and who had reached that level of education. She was nothing short of inspiring.

When I walked into her office for the first time, it felt like a cozy, welcoming space, filled with books neatly stacked on shelves and papers organized in trays. Her degrees hung proudly on the wall next to her desk, each one a reminder of what persistence can achieve. Dr. Garcia had short, curly, dark brown hair and wore glasses that gave her a wise, thoughtful look. That day, she wore a beige pant suit that made her look both professional and approachable. Everything about her, her posture, her presence, her energy, radiated confidence.

She greeted me with genuine enthusiasm, and I could tell she was just as excited to meet another Latina pursuing higher education. Early in our conversation, she asked me what had motivated me to pursue my degree.

"No es muy común for Latinos to pursue higher education," she said gently, acknowledging a reality I knew all too well.

"I know," I replied, shrugging. "Pero mis padres siempre me dijeron que educación es la clave. They never had the chance, so they wanted me to have it."

She nodded, her eyes lighting up. "Exactamente. That's why it is so important, que nos apoyemos entre nosotras."

She leaned forward. "I get that, mija. Pero you have to remember, you're not alone. Siempre hay alguien que can guide you, give you consejos, or just be there to listen."

I smiled, feeling a mix of relief and motivation. "Gracias... it really helps to hear that."

"Siempre, siempre," she said warmly. "Y never forget, your story, tu esfuerzo, puede inspire other chicas detrás de ti. Cada paso que tú das, you're opening doors for someone más."

I opened up about my background, my parents' sacrifices, and the values they had instilled in me: hard work, resilience, and the belief that education could open doors they never had the chance to walk through.

We connected instantly. We had an unspoken understanding in shared culture, language, and struggles. As a fellow Latina, she not only understood the significance of pursuing a degree but also the cultural expectations and emotional weight that often came with it, especially for someone juggling school, work, and caregiving. She reminded me that taking care of myself, physically, mentally, and academically, was not selfish but necessary.

Before we parted ways that day, she looked at me and said, "I'm here for you. Whatever you need, consider me a resource." Those words stayed with me. Knowing I had someone like Dr. Garcia in my corner, someone who had walked a path similar to mine and carved out space for herself in academia, made my time at the university that much sweeter. It reminded me that I wasn't alone, and that there was space for people like me in rooms I once thought were off-limits.

A year into university, I received a phone call at 3 a.m. on a Wednesday. It was the transplant coordinator.

"Hi, is this Rosario?"

"Yes" I responded half asleep.

"We have a kidney for your mom." She said, her voice filled with delight.

I sat up, "Really? That's great!"

"Yes! We need her at UCSD Medical Center immediately."

"Understood. We'll head out soon."

My entire body filled with overwhelming gratitude, and tears of joy streamed down my face. I couldn't believe it. This was the moment we had been waiting and praying for. Since my mom was living with my brother. I called them both immediately, still shaking from the news. The calls were going straight to voicemail so I kept calling until my brother answered.

"Hello?" he mumbled half asleep.

"Wake up! The transplant coordinator called, they have a kidney for mom!"

"What? No way!"

"Yes, but we need to get her to UCSD immediately. Wake her up. I'm getting dressed right now and I'll meet you there, hurry!"

We were all filled with excitement, but underneath it was a layer of nerves. I could see the worry in my mom's eyes, and I felt it in my chest too. This was a major surgery, full of risks, it was not guaranteed that this would work, and in the worst case, she could die during the surgery. However, we were hopeful it was going to work. A second chance at life, not dependent on dialysis three times a week. As we talked and prepared, my mom held tightly to her faith. She said, "Si Dios quiere que esto sea para mí, entonces lo aceptaré con gusto." If God believed this kidney was meant for her, she would accept it wholeheartedly. Her strength embedded in her faith gave all of us a sense of peace.

After they took her back to surgery, I stepped into the hallway and called my work to let them know I wouldn't be coming in. This time, my new supervisor's response surprised me; she was genuinely happy for me. "This is great news," she said. "Take all the time you need." Her support lifted a weight I hadn't realized I was still carrying. For once, I didn't feel scared of losing my job for choosing my family. I could finally be fully present in this moment.

My brother and I stayed by my mom's side, holding her hand as we waited. She was in a mint green hospital gown with the IV line connected to her left arm. When the nurses came to take her to the operating room, we leaned over to hug her tightly and kiss her cheek.

"Everything is going to be fine, mami." I said. "We'll be here when you wake up."

"We love you," My brother added.

"I love you too," She said in a soft tone.

Then came the waiting. Minutes seemed to crawl by, each feeling heavier than the previous, as my stomach twisted into knots and my hands fidgeted. My chest felt tight as

I watched the clock tick impossibly slowly. Finally, by evening, the doctors called us in. The words "the surgery went well" hit me like a wave, and relief washed over me. When we were allowed to see her, she lay in the hospital bed, still under anesthesia, her eyelids fluttering as if she were caught between dreams and reality. The soft beeping of the monitors and the rustling of nurses' gowns filled the room, but my attention was solely on her, delicate yet starting the gradual journey of recovery.

Now, all we could do was wait again, this time to see how her body would respond to the transplant. We didn't know what the days ahead would bring, but for that moment, we held on to hope.

A few days passed, and things were looking promising. Her body was accepting the transplant, and we were filled with a deep sense of relief and overwhelming gratitude. For the first time in a long time, hope didn't feel so far away.

As her condition began to improve, we turned our attention to the next steps. The doctors and nurses carefully walked us through her new post-transplant care routine. The medication list was extensive, and at first, it felt overwhelming. Although she was living with my brother, I became her primary caregiver since I had attended all of the appointments and preparation classes.

I needed to understand every detail, dosages, schedules, and potential side effects. I organized pill bottles, set alarms, and reviewed instructions repeatedly, knowing that her life depended on getting it right, because in many ways, it truly did.

They also trained me on how to administer her insulin injections. Even though I was scared I'd mess it up, I pushed that fear aside and focused. There was no room for doubt, only determination. It was a lot to take in, but I reminded myself that this kidney transplant was a second chance for my mom, for us.

After ten long days in the hospital, my mom was finally discharged, and she left with a stack of follow-up instructions, a bag full of new medications, and a future that suddenly felt possible again.

The first three months after the transplant were the most critical. I took family leave from work so I could be fully present for my mom's recovery. At school, I informed my professors about what was happening at home. To my surprise and deep relief, they were incredibly understanding. Their compassion lifted a weight off my shoulders. I had feared falling behind or even failing, but instead, they gave me the flexibility I needed, offering makeup tests and allowing me to turn in assignments a bit late. For the first time in a long time, I didn't feel like I was drowning under pressure. I felt seen.

Still, emotionally, I was stretched thin. The first few weeks were the hardest. My mom was weak, and the reality of how fragile her recovery could be sank in quickly. I was constantly watching over her, waking up in the middle of the night to check if she was okay. I didn't allow myself much rest.

I woke up around six each morning to give her the first round of medication, which had to be taken one hour before breakfast. I took her vitals and carefully wrote them down before moving to the kitchen to prepare breakfast. Some days I made oatmeal with berries; other days, eggs with toast. She didn't have much of an appetite during those first weeks, but I made sure she ate something. Before she started eating, I checked her blood sugar and injected her insulin.

Once breakfast was over, I cleaned up and encouraged her to move a little. We tried walking down the street, though some days she could only make it to the end of the driveway before needing to rest. After she recovered her energy, it was time to prepare lunch and check her vitals again. We ate, I administered her insulin, and once more I encouraged her to get up and move. The same routine repeated itself again at dinner.

On days when we had appointments at the medical center, we left around 6 a.m. to beat the morning traffic. We arrived early for her bloodwork, waiting until it was finished before she could take her first medications of the day and then wait another hour before eating.

Every day carried the same weight of responsibility, making sure medications were taken on time, monitoring her blood sugar, tracking her vitals, and managing doctor visits. I was operating in survival mode, running on adrenaline and hope.

For the first month, we went to the hospital three times a

week for bloodwork and post-transplant tests. The early mornings, constant driving, and endless appointments blurred together, leaving little time to rest or reset. I carried folders filled with medical paperwork, medication lists, and questions for the doctors; always afraid I might forget something important. Every lab result felt like it held our future in its hands, and the responsibility of getting everything right weighed heavily on me. The fear of complications never fully left my mind: one abnormal number, one missed symptom, one mistake could change everything.

There were moments when I cried alone in my car, gripping the steering wheel, releasing the tears I didn't allow myself to show in front of her. I was physically drained, emotionally stretched, and constantly afraid of failing her, yet determined to hold it together. I reminded myself that this was what love looked like, this was what sacrifice felt like.

By the second month, her appointments were reduced to twice a week. I started noticing her energy returning, her color improving. Seeing those little signs of healing gave me the strength to keep going. I was still tired, still juggling everything, but beneath the exhaustion was gratitude. We were finally moving forward.

Things had been running smoothly, at least as smoothly as they could, until one afternoon after a hospital visit. We were driving home when I noticed the temperature gauge on my car's dashboard creeping up. My car was overheating. Panic started to rise in my chest, but I tried to stay calm.

Thankfully, we were almost home. Still, the moment we pulled into the driveway, a wave of dread hit me. Great. One more thing. Just when I thought I was getting a handle on everything, life threw another curveball.

I asked my neighbor to take a quick look at it since I didn't know the first thing about cars. He checked the fluids and the basics but suggested I take it to a mechanic to be sure. And just like that, my mind started racing: another unexpected expense, money I didn't have. I was already on family leave, receiving only a portion of my salary—just enough to scrape by. I was covering groceries, gas, and every cost that came with caring for my mom and driving her to appointments. There was no room in the budget for car repairs.

When the mechanic told me the radiator needed to be replaced, and it would cost $2,000, I felt the anxiety grip my body. My stomach dropped, churning violently, and my hands felt cold and sweaty. How am I supposed to pay for this? Why now? I felt like I couldn't catch a break. I needed that car to take my mom to her checkups. I was already stretched thin emotionally and financially. This wasn't just a car issue, it was a lifeline issue. And now, even that felt like it was slipping through my fingers, leaving me hollow and powerless, my pulse thudding in my ears as the reality of our fragility pressed down on me.

I felt completely defeated. How was I going to make this work? My closest lifeline, my brother, wasn't available, away at a training. The weight of everything hit me all at once, and in that moment, I was reminded of something

I already knew, but this time, it echoed louder than ever: Nobody was coming to save me. No matter what happened, no matter how impossible things felt, I had to figure it out.

I always did. I always had to.

The mechanic wiped his hands on a rag and looked at me carefully.

"You might want to start thinking about getting a new car," he said. "This is probably just the beginning. Once these issues start, more usually follow."

My stomach sank. Honestly, I didn't have the bandwidth to deal with more problems, or the money to fix them.

Frustrated and overwhelmed, I called a friend I had made at work and vented. "I don't know how I'm supposed to handle one more thing right now," I told her. "My mom's recovery, the hospital visits, and now my car might give out on me."

She listened patiently before saying, "You know, my husband knows someone at a car dealership. He might be able to help you get a good deal.".

I left the mechanic shop and drove straight to the dealership to meet my friend and her husband, hoping I could trade in my car and use it as a down payment. I didn't want a new car, not with everything else going on, but I needed something reliable. My mom's care depended on it. I didn't care what color it was or what model; I needed a car that would start every morning and get us where we needed to go.

Thankfully, the dealership accepted my car as a down payment. The salesperson ran my credit, and I held my breath. I had no idea where my credit stood. My mind flashed back to the times I had maxed out my cards, drowning in bills I didn't know how to manage. But over the past few years, I had learned the hard way: paying off balances on time, tracking expenses, and budgeting carefully. Those lessons, earned through mistakes and persistence, were finally paying off. To my surprise and relief, my credit score was over 700, which qualified me for their promotional, 1% interest rate.

My new car payment would be $250 a month. I sighed at the thought of taking on another expense. I was already living on a tight budget, and now it would be even tighter. But I reminded myself why I was doing it: for my mom, for her kidney, for her life. At least now, I could continue taking her to her appointments without the constant fear of breaking down.

As I pulled out of the dealership lot in my new Toyota Corolla, I felt a strange mix of pride and exhaustion. This wasn't the life I had imagined, but it was the one I was living, moment by moment, doing the best I could with what I had. I didn't have a safety net. There were no shortcuts. But I had my determination, my hope, and my "why". And somehow, even when everything felt like too much, I always found a way.

Years later, as I sit and write this, I still drive that car. It's practical, reliable, and there's no reason to get a new one if this one still works. When I drove away from the dealership that day, I promised myself I would keep it until it couldn't run anymore. It's still a reminder of the persistence that carried us forward.

This chapter of our lives was far from over, but I was learning that even in chaos, I could create stability one decision, one sacrifice, one victory at a time. And just when I thought I couldn't carry more, something incredible happened. After years of balancing caregiving, work, and school, I was finally nearing the finish line.

Graduation was around the corner.

Chapter 9

Living the Dream

A few months after my mom's transplant, things finally began to settle. Her appointments became less frequent—just routine check-ups to monitor her progress. With the constant trips to the hospital behind us, I could breathe a little easier and start shifting my focus back to school. It wasn't that the weight was gone, but it was finally manageable.

I was going to school full-time and still working part-time. Some days, the load felt unbearable—long nights filled with readings, papers, and group projects, followed by early mornings rushing to work. But I kept pushing. I held tightly to one vision that kept me going: walking across that graduation stage. That image was like a lighthouse for me. No matter how tired I was, I could see it in the distance. I checked my academic portal regularly, counting down the number of credits I needed. As it got closer, I decided to take five classes in one semester, something I had never done before, so I could get to graduation that much faster. I wasn't aiming for straight A's. I wanted good grades, of course, but more than anything, I just needed to cross that finish line. At that point in my journey, perfection wasn't the goal; survival was.

Throughout my academic career, I was never a straight-A student. In fact, I never really thought I was smart enough to be one. I carried that belief for years. Looking back now, I realize I had too much on my mind to obsess over perfect grades. Too many real-life responsibilities were weighing on me outside the classroom. Between caregiving, working, managing bills, and just trying to stay afloat emotionally, "getting by" was already a huge win. And yet, I was getting closer to the degree I once thought was out of reach.

What kept me going wasn't academic perfection, it was purpose. I wasn't doing this just for me. I was doing it for my mom, my dad, for my younger self, for every sacrifice that had brought me to this point.

As I approached my final semester at the university, I submitted my graduation application. I had double-checked my credits, and I knew I had enough to graduate, but that familiar voice of self-doubt crept in. What if something's missing? What if they don't accept it? I had come so far, but the fear of something going wrong still lingered. By now, you'd think I would've learned not to give those thoughts so much power, but they always seemed to find a way in, whispering worst-case scenarios just when I was about to reach a milestone.

Then, the email came. My application was accepted. I stared at the screen in disbelief, my heart pounding. I was really going to graduate.

Before I could stop them, tears ran down my face. I had finally made it to the finish line. After years of going to school part-time, working, caring for my mom, managing bills, and simply trying to survive, I made it. I was finally at the finish line, a dream I had nurtured for so long during long nights at the kitchen table with textbooks and empty coffee cups, and on the days I raced from class to work, and then to my mom's appointments. It was no longer just a dream. It was real. It was happening. This email, at this moment, was proof that persistence mattered, that even when I was exhausted, even when I was afraid, it was worth continuing. Somehow, despite the moments when it felt like everyone else had it easier, that I was falling behind while life asked too much of me, I made it. I was going to be a college graduate.

With tears of joy still streaming down my face, the first person I called was my mom. "¡Lo logré, mamá!" I said, my voice cracking with emotion. I did it.

There was a pause, and then her voice, full of pride and love, came through: "Lo hiciste, mijita. Después de todo tu esfuerzo... ya sabía que lo ibas a hacer." You did it, darling. After all your effort... I knew you were going to do it.

Hearing her say that broke me in the best way. She knew. She had witnessed every step, every late night, every tear, every moment I doubted myself.

After I hung up, I called my dad, and he was just as proud. "Estoy tan orgulloso de ti," he said. I'm so proud of you. In that moment, their voices, their joy made everything I had carried feel a little lighter. And then, after I hung up the phone, I sat in silence, letting it all sink in.

I thought about how neither of my parents had the opportunity to go to college. And neither did their parents. I had come from a long line of hardworking, resilient people who were laborers and survivors. For them, education was not a given, it was a luxury that was just out of reach.

I thought about my grandmothers: married young, raising children in difficult homes, surviving domestic violence like their mothers before them. Their lives had been defined by sacrifice, by roles they didn't choose. But through all that pain, they passed down strength.

I imagined how proud they would be if they saw me now that I hadn't married young, that I had no children at that point–not because I didn't want them, but because I had a choice—and that I had the freedom to dream and to prepare myself to walk across a graduation stage they never got to step on.

In that moment, I realized this dream wasn't just mine, it belonged to my parents, my grandparents, my ancestors, the women who had to quiet their voices so that one day, someone like me could use hers. This graduation was for every woman who endured in silence; every ancestor who worked the fields, cleaned houses, or bent over sewing machines; every dream deferred. I was filled with gratitude, with pride, with purpose. This wasn't just a degree, it was a generational win.

The morning of my graduation, I got ready with a heart full of excitement. As I looked at my cap and gown, it felt like I was about to wear the most beautiful dress of my life.

I got in my car and drove to the university, every moment of that ride etched in my memory like it happened yesterday. The sky was overcast, a typical "May Gray" morning in Southern California, but I didn't mind. Nothing could dull my joy.

I had an upbeat playlist blasting through the speakers to match my energy. Then "Titanium" featuring Sia came on. As the chorus played, "You shoot me down, but I won't fall..." something in me stirred. It was the perfect anthem for the day. It was a reminder that no matter what life threw at me, I didn't fall. I had proven that to myself over and over. Tears of joy started to roll down my face, but I quickly wiped them away. I didn't want to show up to graduation looking like I had been crying, but inside, I was overflowing with pride, gratitude, and disbelief. To this day, whenever I hear that song, it instantly takes me back to that drive.

I pulled into campus alongside a sea of graduates, the nervous yet joyful energy practically buzzing in the air. All around me, graduates were fixing their black caps and adjusting their gowns, hugging friends, smoothing out wrinkles, taking pictures, double-checking their tassels, and soaking in the moment they had all worked so hard for.

As I lined up for the procession, I could feel the tears welling up again, but I held them back. No one else around me was crying, and I didn't want to be the only one showing that much emotion. I glanced around and noticed that many of the students looked younger than me. I knew that for most of them, this journey had only taken four years, and all without working full-time jobs, or caregiving, or navigating life's obstacles the way I had. A part of me thought about the luxury they had, the smoother road. But I quickly reminded myself: my path may have been longer, but I never gave up. I kept going, one step at a time. Any progress I made, no matter how slow, was still progress.

And here I was. I made it.

"Pomp and Circumstance" began to play—our cue to walk in. The moment those first notes filled the air, I felt a wave of emotion rush over me. My eyes were brimming with tears, and goosebumps covered my arms. I quickly wiped my tears and stepped forward with my chin up and huge smile.

I made it to my seat and anxiously waited for the speeches to finish, counting down the moments until I would hear my name. In my mind, I was replaying the same vision I had imagined over and over again: me walking across that stage. I was just moments away from turning that dream into a reality.

Then, they began to call names. My row stood up, and we slowly moved toward the stage. I climbed the steps, heart pounding, and before I knew it, I heard: "Rosario Aranda."

I walked across the stage feeling proud and grateful with a smile on my face.

In the distance, I heard cheering, it was faint, but I knew it was my family. That was enough.

After the ceremony there was chaos. Crowds of graduates and their loved ones filled the space, and I searched desperately for my family. It took a while, but when we finally found each other in the crowd, I ran straight into my mom's arms.

"Sí se pudo, mami," I whispered. We did it, mom. She hugged me tightly, and I could feel the pride radiating from her. I turned to my dad and hugged him, his eyes filled with tears.

"Estoy muy orgulloso de ti," he said. I'm so proud of you.

My brother and his family were there too, greeting me with big smiles and warm hugs. It was the first time we had all been together as a family since I moved out, which made the event even more special.

In that moment, I felt satisfaction and pride I had never experienced before. Their joy made all the sacrifices worth it. To this day, it remains the proudest moment of my life, because I didn't give up and became the first in my family to graduate from college.

That day was more than just about a diploma. It was about reclaiming every "no se puede" and turning it into "sí se pudo." It was about proving to myself, and to every woman who came before me, that the sacrifices weren't in vain.

Graduation was more than a ceremony. It was a declaration that I belonged, that I was capable, and that I could rise, even when the odds were stacked against me.

This marked the end of one chapter, but, more importantly, the beginning of a new one. In this new chapter, I would carry my family's strength, my own resilience, and a sense of purpose into whatever came next. And I knew that whatever challenges lay ahead, I would hold onto my vision, my clear picture of what I wanted my future to be. In the hardest moments, when doubt crept in and the path felt impossible, that vision would guide me forward, reminding me of my strength, my worth, and the extraordinary things I can achieve.

Chapter 10

In Search of a Meaningful Career

Now that I had my degree, I was ready to start searching for a meaningful career. My time in the banking industry taught me many lessons; it kept me financially afloat while I finished school and helped shape my professional foundation. At the bank, I learned more than just how to handle money. I gained insight into the financial world, from budgeting to understanding what a 401(k) and a Roth IRA were—things I was never taught at home or school. I heard about investments for the first time. Beyond financial knowledge, I built valuable skills: I strengthened my customer service skills, learned to multitask, hit sales goals, and performed under pressure. But the most valuable lesson I learned was to advocate for myself and realize my self-worth.

My parents taught me the value of hard work, how to keep my head down, do my job well, and be grateful for every opportunity. Growing up, I heard the saying "calladita te ves mas bonita," that girls are prettier when they're quiet. So speaking up or advocating for oneself wasn't something my parents were familiar with, and for a long time, neither was I.

For a few years, I kept my head down, worked hard, and met all of my sales goals thinking that I would get recognized for my hard work. That was what my parents had taught me about work ethic. Then one day my boss unexpectedly called me into his office.

"We're so happy with your recent accomplishments and how you've been meeting your goals," he said. "We'd like to offer you a promotion."

I was overwhelmed with pride, thinking that all of my hard work was finally getting recognized. I held back tears and, and, with a big smile, I replied, "Yes, thank you so much." He smiled back and told me HR would reach out later that day to go over the pay and paperwork. As I waited for the call, I daydreamed about what the raise might look like, thinking about the bills I could pay and what I could possibly start saving.

When someone from HR called, they explained the forms I'd need to sign and then shared the salary. My excitement immediately faded. They were offering me the lowest pay in the range and not a penny more.

I asked if there was room to negotiate. They said they would need to check with my boss. The next day, they called back to tell me my boss had declined my request. I felt defeated. I questioned whether I should even accept the promotion, but I did, because I thought I should be grateful for the opportunity.

In the days that followed, I couldn't stop thinking about

it. It didn't sit right with me. I felt undervalued; this wasn't nearly what I should be getting paid. Should I start looking for another job? Should I ask again? Then a terrifying thought crossed my mind: What if I emailed my boss's boss asking if I could renegotiate? The idea scared me. What if it backfired? What if I lost my job?

Still, I couldn't shake the feeling that staying silent would haunt me more than trying. I wrote the email asking if I could renegotiate at a later time. After I finished writing it, I stared at my screen, debating whether or not to hit send. Instead, I saved it. Then the next day, I couldn't stop thinking about it. What if they say no? What if they say yes? What if I regret not trying? I found the courage to finally hit send.

Days passed without a response. My mind imagined every possible negative outcome: being labeled "difficult", losing my job, being left without income. I had to constantly remind myself not to jump ahead.

Then I saw the email.

My heart dropped as I opened it, bracing for the worst. Instead, he wrote, "Let me look into this, and I'll get back to you." I replied with a simple, "Thank you."

A few more days passed. Then my phone rang.

"Hello, this is Rosario."

"Hi Rosario, this is the HR Director. I'm calling to let you know we're increasing your pay to the midpoint of the range, and we'll be providing back pay as well."

I sighed in relief before the excitement hit. "Thank you so much."

When I hung up, tears rolled down my face. I wasn't just relieved, I was proud. I was proud I went against everything I was taught to believe about staying quiet and being grateful, proud that I spoke up.

That experience taught me a lesson I carry with me to this day: advocating for yourself isn't being ungrateful, it's recognizing your worth. If I hadn't spoken up for myself then, no one else would have. Advocating for myself felt unfamiliar and uncomfortable. I was filled with doubt and fear but writing that email taught me to stand up for myself. I learned to use my voice and to change the narrative I grew up with, that we are prettier when we speak, especially when we stand up for ourselves.

The bank helped me become financially literate and taught me valuable lessons in customer service, but it also gave me a glimpse into the uglier parts of humanity. One day, when I refused to cash a check because the account didn't have enough funds, a woman lashed out at me, telling me to "go back to my country". I was boiling inside. I tried to stay calm, but I also wasn't going to stay silent. In a firm voice, I told her, "You should read a history book. Mexicans were here first." She didn't expect me to give it back so she started cursing at me. We called the police, and she was escorted out.

Sadly, this experience wasn't new to me. I had grown up hearing my parents talk about the discrimination they faced. As a first-gen, racism is something many of us grow up witnessing, either directly or through the stories our families carry. That moment reminded me just how deep those wounds can go.

After that, I knew it was time to close that chapter. I had gained what I needed—real-world experience, financial literacy, and thicker skin—but I was ready to find a career that aligned more with my purpose, something in the nonprofit or government sector where I could serve my community and create change.

I started job hunting, but I was completely burnt out from working at the bank. Now that school was over, I took on more hours to save as much as I could because I was planning to quit even if I didn't have another job lined up. I felt confident that with my degree in hand, I'd be able to find something new. I had saved enough to cover a couple of months of expenses, so I finally gave my notice.

To stretch my savings, I kept my spending low. At the time, I was still living with roommates, which helped keep rent affordable. I threw myself into the job search, attending networking events, job fairs, and applying online. I got a couple of calls for interviews, but none of them turned into offers. I was hopeful after each one, but the callbacks never came.

Each rejection, or worse, each silence, chipped away at my excitement. I had worked so hard for my degree, and yet here I was, months later, with no clear next step. It was discouraging. I felt like I was falling behind again, like the promise of a better future that came with earning a college degree was slipping through my fingers. I kept wondering if I had made a mistake. Were all those late nights studying and student loans worth it?

As weeks turned into months and my savings dwindled, I had no choice but to start applying to banking jobs again. Thankfully, with my experience, I was able to land something quickly, but I knew I didn't want to stay there long. Every lunch break, I'd sit in my car, eating and scrolling through job announcements on my phone. This became my routine. I applied to nonprofit roles, hoping to pivot into meaningful work, but I never heard back.

Then one day, I came across a job posting for a finance role at a government agency. It felt like a potential foot in the door, a stepping stone to something bigger. I applied and soon received an invitation to take a written exam. There were no study guides provided, but since the role was finance-related, I started practicing basic math, without a calculator.

When I arrived on test day, it looked like there were over 100 people there. A wave of fear and self-doubt washed over me. Was I really going to score high enough to beat all these people? I gave myself a pep talk right there in the lobby. "I've made it this far. I'm not stopping now. I'm getting to the next round."

The test lasted two hours, and I walked out feeling defeated, like this opportunity was slipping through my fingers. For the next few days, I checked my email constantly, hoping for an interview invitation.

A week later, I got the email that I had an interview, and luckily, it was scheduled on my day off from the bank. I immediately went into preparation mode. Every day after work, I researched interview tips online, crafted my responses to potential questions, and practiced saying them out loud. I did everything I could to make it to the next round.

On the day of the interview, I wore my best professional outfit: black pants, a blue blouse, and a black blazer. I walked in feeling confident, trying not to listen to the doubt in my head. I arrived early and waited patiently until they called me in.

Three interviewers sat across from me. It felt so official, unlike anything I had experienced before. They asked me ten questions, and I answered them just as I had practiced. The time flew by, but I walked out knowing I had given it my all.

The next day, I kept my phone within reach, hoping for a callback to tell me I had made it to the second round. When it finally came, I was so excited, it finally felt like I was getting closer to the career my parents and I had dreamed about.

The second interview was with two people and felt a bit easier than the first since they asked fewer questions. At the end, they told me there would be one final interview with the finance director. A few days later, I got a call to schedule it. I was nervous but more confident—I had made it this far, and for the first time, I felt like I really had a chance.

On the day of the interview, I wore black pants, a blouse, and a blazer I had picked up from Ross. The interview itself was short, only about fifteen minutes. He asked a couple of questions I had already encountered in the previous rounds, so I knew exactly how to respond. I had never gone through so many interviews for a single position, and somehow, each one had fallen on my day off, as if it were meant to be.

A week after my third interview, HR called with a job offer. I was over the moon; this was the moment I had worked so hard for, and I accepted immediately. The pay was higher than what I had earned at the bank, and it came with a full benefits package, including health insurance—something my parents had never had. And the best part? I wouldn't have to work weekends anymore.

It wasn't just a new position, I was working for a government agency, which meant I was contributing to something bigger than myself. I would be serving the very community I lived in. In a way, it felt like I was giving back to the people and the places that were shaping me. And now, I had the chance to pay it forward. Plus, this was the job my parents had always dreamed of for themselves, one that didn't require being on my feet all day, doing hard manual labor that left my body aching. I had a job with a desk, a nameplate, a steady paycheck, health insurance, a retirement plan, and paid time off. Now this job my parents had dreamed of for themselves was mine. It was proof that the long hours, the missed meals, the worries, all their sacrifices had not been in vain.

I called my mom to share the good news, and the joy in her voice was instant. "¡Mi hija! Dios escuchó nuestras oraciones," she exclaimed. "Every night I whispered your name to God and lit a veladora, asking Him to open doors for you. And now… look at you!" I could hear her smiling through the phone, her words wrapping me in warmth and relief. "I knew it would happen," she added softly, "you just had to keep going.".

My parents didn't have a network of connections or influential friends to call on; what they had was faith, and they clung to it like a lifeline. When I called my dad, his voice carried the same excitement. "Mija, this is the perfect job," he said. "You'll have benefits, a retirement plan, everything we dreamed you'd one day have."

When I hung up the phone with my parents, I just sat there in silence for a moment, letting it all sink in. I thought about everything it took to get here, the long nights studying after work, the rejection emails, the interviews I didn't get. Now, I was stepping into something entirely new. I was about to become the first in my family to work in an office. My parents had spent their lives in jobs that kept them on their feet all day, lifting heavy things, working under the sun, or standing behind a counter. I was going to sit at a desk, use a computer, and be paid for what I knew, rather than for how much my body could endure.

My first year in my new career was full of learning and reflection. One of the things that stood out to me was the offices with framed bachelor's degrees, master's degrees, and even a couple of doctorates hanging on the walls. After graduating, I knew firsthand how challenging that path was. I was still carrying nearly $50,000 in debt, so the idea of going back to school felt overwhelming. I didn't want to add more debt, yet seeing those degrees planted a seed in my mind. It reminded me of something my mom used to say growing up: "Dime con quién andas y te diré quién eres." Tell me who you hang out with, and I'll tell you who you are. When I worked at the bank, nobody around me had advanced degrees, and it wasn't even on my radar. But now, surrounded by people who had achieved so much academically, the possibility began to feel real and, for the first time, attainable.

One day, I was walking past the finance manager's office and couldn't help but stop to admire the degrees on his wall. He noticed me staring and asked, "Rosario, are you thinking about getting a master's degree?" I hesitated and admitted, "I don't think someone like me could ever do that." I had never considered myself smart enough for grad school, I felt like I had barely made it through undergrad.

He smiled and said something that stuck with me: "I wasn't the smartest kid or the brightest in the class, and if I can do it, you can do it." Those words lingered in my mind long after that moment, and for the first time, I began to seriously consider that maybe, just maybe, it was possible for me too.

I also couldn't help but notice that there weren't many Latinos working there, and among the degrees I saw, none belonged to Latinos. The first time I walked into the annual holiday party, the lack of representation was clear. I felt like a minority in that space, but I also felt proud to be there, knowing I was opening doors, even in ways that weren't immediately visible.

My first year taught me that simply being in the room mattered, but it also taught me that I didn't want to stop there. Every time I walked past those walls lined with diplomas, I was reminded that education was still a powerful key, not just for opening doors but for keeping them open. I had already broken barriers by being the first in my family to work in an office, but I began to wonder what else I could achieve if I kept going. The thought of earning my own advanced degree started as a whisper in the back of my mind, but by the end of that year, it had become a goal I couldn't ignore.

Chapter 11

The Eight Percent

After a few years in my position, I started searching for promotional opportunities within the organization. I would go to interviews, but I never made it past the first round. Each rejection stung, not just because I wanted to grow, but because I felt like I was hitting an invisible ceiling. I had pushed myself to reach this point, and yet the next step always seemed out of reach.

Part of the frustration came from knowing how few people who looked like me—Latinas, first-generation students, women from humble beginnings—were in positions of leadership. It wasn't just me facing barriers; it was a reflection of a system where representation was scarce. I thought about my mentor at the university, Dr. Garcia, one of the few Latinas with a Ph.D., and the example she set made me realize both the rarity of such representation and how crucial it is.

I knew I needed to set myself apart from everyone else, a way to break through the barriers and make my own path in spaces where so few had walked before me.

The thought of going back to school kept surfacing, but I didn't feel ready financially. Then something unexpected happened. Our HR department announced a special program in partnership with San Diego State University, exclusively for employees, to earn a master's in public administration. In this program, each course would last eight weeks, and professors would come directly to our office building to teach after work. The best part was the generous tuition reimbursement program, which meant I would only pay 20% of the tuition. It was a huge relief. I was still paying off my student loans, and this program would keep me from adding even more debt.

Even though I didn't have a clear path forward toward obtaining a master's, this opportunity reminded me that sometimes the way finds you. Life has a way of opening doors when you least expect it, and this felt like one of those rare moments. It was an invitation to step forward, to take a chance, and to trust that the path would become clear as I moved along with it. It felt like an opportunity that didn't come around twice. This could be my chance to finally earn a master's degree, break through that ceiling, and prove to myself and to others that I could go further than I had ever imagined.

I eagerly gathered everything I needed for the application: GRE scores, letters of recommendation, and my personal statement. Once I submitted it all, the waiting began, and like always, the voices of doubt crept in. What if I don't get accepted? What if I'm the only one in my cohort who doesn't make it in?

Since all of my prospective classmates were colleagues from work, we checked in every day to see if anyone had heard back. Then one day, a colleague messaged me: "Check your email." My heart raced as I opened it, and there it was. I had been accepted into the program.

I felt an overwhelming mix of excitement and pride, but alongside the joy was the awareness that I was standing at the base of a very tall mountain. This time, though, I wanted the climb to be different from my undergraduate experience. I didn't want to just get by. I wanted to thrive. I was in a stronger place now: I had a stable job where I felt supported, I was doing okay financially, and my mom's health was stable. I began mentally preparing for the journey ahead, asking myself what I could do differently to make sure I succeeded. For the first time, I set a bold academic goal: straight A's.

To stay focused, I deleted all of my social media accounts. I wasn't going to let distractions steal my time. I also promised myself I wouldn't procrastinate like before. At the start of the semester, I made a list of my classes and wrote an "A" next to each one. I pinned that list to my desk, where I would see it every day. I was ready, not just to be a grad student, but to become the student I had always wanted to be.

At the start of 2019, I began my grad school journey. Classes were held on Thursday evenings, which worked perfectly. I could spend my weekends focusing on homework and have everything wrapped up before Sunday night.

Our first course was an introduction to public administration. One of the early assignments was to give a presentation in front of the class. I was nervous. I had taken a public speaking course before, but at that moment, it felt like I had forgotten everything I'd learned. On top of that, I felt extra, self-imposed pressure to do well because I was presenting to colleagues. What if I messed up? What if they didn't take me seriously? What if I embarrassed myself?

As I walked to the front of the room, my palms were sweaty, and anxiety swirled in my stomach. Still, I pushed through. I spoke for ten minutes about ethics in public services, earned an A, and felt relieved, but I knew my delivery could have been stronger. I stumbled over a few words, my voice wavered in places, and I filled the gaps with too many "ums" and "ahs," which distracted from the content of my presentation.

That night, I started thinking about how to improve my public speaking. I remembered hearing at work about a public speaking club called Toastmasters. That weekend, I looked it up. The idea of walking into a meeting intimidated me, but my desire to improve was stronger than my fear.

This wasn't just about getting a good grade. As a first-generation Latina in a professional setting, I knew how rare it was to see someone like me standing at the front of a room, speaking with authority. Public speaking wasn't just a skill; it was a way to claim space in places where my community was often underrepresented.

By the end of our graduate program, we would have twenty minutes to deliver a presentation on a capstone project of our choice. I didn't just want mine to be good; I wanted it to inspire confidence in me as a professional and as a representative of my community. I had two years to prepare. That became my new goal: to master the skill of public speaking and nail that presentation, not just for myself, but for everyone who had paved the way for me to stand in that room.

I found a Toastmasters club nearby that met on Wednesday nights, but it took me months to work up the courage to attend my first meeting. When I finally walked in, it was nothing like I had imagined. I had pictured rows of stiff chairs, a room full of serious, suited speakers, and everyone silently judging each other, but it was the complete opposite. I arrived about ten minutes early and walked into a retirement home where the Toastmasters group met in a small conference room. I was greeted by someone who smiled, asked for my name, and shook my hand. He walked me into the room and handed me an agenda for the meeting. Everyone was dressed in regular clothes— not suits—and they were standing around, smiling and chatting with each other. I noticed right away that it was a diverse group of people of different ages and backgrounds. Several members came up to welcome me and gave me an overview of what to expect. Their warm welcome eased my nerves.

I was pleasantly surprised by the diversity in the group, including other Latinas. Members were at all different stages of their public speaking journey: some spoke with the polish of seasoned professionals, while others, like me, were just starting out. The atmosphere felt safe and supportive, a place where I could learn, practice, and receive constructive feedback without judgment. Each Toastmasters meeting follows a simple structure: opportunities to practice impromptu speaking, to deliver prepared speeches, and receive thoughtful feedback designed to help each speaker grow.

At that moment, I knew I had found the right place to grow. I became a member and committed to attending meetings every Wednesday evening. What I didn't realize at the time was just how much this decision would positively shape not only my public speaking skills and my confidence, but also my career and the way I carried myself in every room I entered. I also had no idea that I would meet one of my mentors, Erica Alfaro, there—the person who would later become part of the inspiration behind my dream of writing a book. I met her just as her career as a keynote speaker was taking off, witnessing all the incredible things she would go on to accomplish, becoming an international keynote speaker and an award-winning author. She was one of the few Latina keynote speakers I had ever seen on conference and university stages. She made me believe in dreams I wasn't sure someone like me could achieve—a powerful reminder that representation matters. She planted that seed long before I ever believed I could make it grow.

I was proud of myself, I was thriving in my grad program, sharpening my public speaking skills, and managing to balance it all. At work, someone encouraged me to find a mentor in the office to help me grow professionally, so I took the leap. I reached out to a woman in a different division whom I deeply admired. Anita was the kind of person who brightened any room with her warmth and friendliness, always ready to lend a hand. I told her I wanted to learn, to shadow her, to grow professionally. She said yes instantly, her enthusiasm matching my own. That was the start of her mentorship. She opened doors to knowledge I didn't even know existed, sharing wisdom from her years in the organization. Everything felt like it was falling into place.

And then, just when life seemed steady, the world stopped.

The pandemic changed everything overnight. Our office adopted a hybrid schedule, with some days at home and others masked and distanced at work. The atmosphere was filled with uncertainty, making adaptability a daily necessity. My mentor and I could no longer meet in person as before, but she refused to let these changes hinder our progress. We transitioned to virtual coffee chats, quick hallway catch-ups on in-office days, and conversations about navigating the chaos. Her mentorship during that time extended beyond career advice; it was a vital support. She reminded me to breathe, stay flexible, and seek opportunities despite the instability around us.

Meanwhile, a persistent fear lingered. My mom had a compromised immune system, which put her at high risk of catching COVID and experiencing serious complications. The thought of her getting sick kept me constantly anxious. Even dropping off groceries felt like a risk, because I could accidentally pass the virus to her, and one simple mistake could put her health in danger.

To avoid being overwhelmed by everything happening globally, I focused on my schoolwork and aimed for good grades. Throughout, I was balancing graduate school, work, and protecting the person I cared about most by masking, sanitizing, and keeping a safe distance from others.

Despite the chaos going on in the world, a pleasant surprise was waiting for me: a promotion and the chance to work with my mentor full-time. It was a reminder that even in the most uncertain seasons, good things could still happen. The role gave me a chance to learn directly from someone I admired, to develop my skills, and to take on more responsibility than I ever had before. Everything was going smoothly. After a few months in my new role, it was time to prepare for my capstone project.

I began the research for my capstone project, the final step before graduation, so close to the finish line. I pored over the paper and met with my professor to ensure it reflected my best work. Then came the twenty-minute presentation. I was a little nervous about presenting, but I reminded myself of all the practice I had put in at Toastmasters for the past year. I must have run through that presentation at least twenty times, visualizing each moment until it felt natural. When the day finally came, my nerves were there, but so was my preparation. As soon as I finished, the positive feedback and compliments flowed in, just as I had envisioned. I felt proud of what I had accomplished, happy that my effort had paid off, and relieved that all the nerves and late nights had been worth it. For the first time in all of my academic journey, I had earned straight A's, a moment that felt like proof I was capable of more than I had ever imagined. Now, the only thing left was walking across the stage, just like I had pictured myself doing.

On graduation morning, my cap and gown hung neatly behind the door, waiting. My heart was a mix of excitement and thoughtful reflection. Because safety protocols were still in place due to the pandemic, we could only invite a limited number of guests. Out of caution, my parents didn't attend, but I knew they were with me in spirit, beaming with pride at this new accomplishment. Instead, my brother and his kids came to celebrate with me. Watching them cheer felt like my parents were there through them, our family's pride carried forward to the next generation.

This graduation felt different from my previous one. My first degree had been a monumental milestone for my family and me, a shared victory for all the sacrifices we had made. But this time...it was personal. In 2021, the Pew Research Center reported that only 8% of Latinas in the US held advanced degrees. Now, I was one of them. That number made me pause. I felt proud but also remembered how far I had come and how rare this accomplishment was for someone like me. I thought of my parents, of the sacrifices that got me here, and of all the first-generation students who might not yet see a path forward.

Earning my master's proved to myself that I could go further than I had ever imagined, that no matter the obstacles, I would always find a way or the way would find me, that I was capable of not just finishing but excelling. I had never considered myself the smartest person in the room, yet grad school gave me the focus and confidence I never had before.

This season of my life wasn't just about academic milestones; it was about transformation in every sense. Around the same time, I was finishing grad school, life surprised me in the most unexpected way: I met the man who would one day become my husband.

Before meeting Johnny, marriage wasn't something I longed for. I hadn't grown up seeing examples of healthy, respectful relationships. To me, marriage seemed difficult, full of challenges. I thought about my parents' relationship; while they weren't affectionate with each other, they did their best to create a loving family.

Along the way, I had my own relationships. Some gave me positive experiences and glimpses of what care and respect could feel like. Others left me with lessons about what I did not want, reminding me of the importance of boundaries and self-worth. Each experience shaped me, little by little, into someone who knew what she was searching for.

Could I have a relationship that felt easy? One grounded in respect, love, and support, and filled with fun and laughter? With Johnny, I envisioned what a long-term partnership might look like, and for the first time, the thought of marriage brought me a sense of hope. I felt grateful for the possibility, joyful at the thought of love done differently.

Everything was coming together. I was stepping into a new chapter, both professionally and personally. I was building my career, proud of my accomplishments, and continuing to practice public speaking, developing the confidence I had once been searching for. I was also starting a healthy, loving relationship. I am proud of myself for not rushing or settling for anything less than I deserved. I had grown into a woman who knew her worth.

Meditation, which had once been my refuge during one of the most stressful seasons of my life, had now become part of my lifestyle. What began as a way to cope had evolved into a daily practice of grounding and gratitude. To this day, I continue to turn to meditation as a way to reconnect with myself, find balance, and return to peace no matter what life brings.

Looking back, little Rosario had been filled with doubt and fear, carrying the weight of her parents' dreams. She would be so proud to see how I always found a way, no matter the obstacle. Every tear, every sleepless night, every challenge I had faced wasn't just for me, it was for my parents, my grandparents, and all of the ancestors who had dreamed of a life they couldn't have. Every sacrifice they made, every barrier they endured, had steadily built the foundation for me to rise. And that journey led me to something bigger than myself. Now I am the one opening doors and setting an example for the next generation.

I feel a deep sense of gratitude and admiration, knowing that I am living a life they could only hope for. Every success, every joy, every step forward was a continuation of their legacy. And in that reflection, I understood I wasn't just building my life, I was honoring the courage, resilience, and dreams of every woman who came before me as well as those who will come after me.

Chapter 7

Dear Little Rosario

Dear little Rosario,

I can see you, sitting there with your backpack, your favorite pink outfit, wearing mom's pink lipstick, so excited to start first grade. You're already imagining all the friends you're going to make, and yes, you will make them.

Please don't shrink when they say your name wrong. Speak up. Correct them. Your name is not a burden, it's a gift. One day you'll realize how special it is, that it carries your abuelita's legacy—her strength, her faith. You'll carry her in every introduction, every room you enter, and you'll be proud.

I know how much you care about school; how much you want to do well. That effort, that hunger to learn, it will carry you so far. Even when it feels unfair, even when Mom and Dad's constant reminders to "study hard" sound like pressure, remember this: They only want the best for you. Their dreams will slowly become your dreams, and you'll work so hard to honor them. You'll even fear letting them down but hear me: You will never disappoint them. They are proud of you already, just for being you.

The confusion you feel about navigating two worlds will get better. You'll start to see this as an advantage instead of a disadvantage. You'll also see how helping Mom and Dad with adult responsibilities is preparing you for what's to come. You are gaining skills like resilience and strength that will help you through tough times.

There will be times when life feels too heavy, moments when you'll want to quit, nights when you'll cry thinking there's no way out, times you'll feel alone and you'll ask yourself, "Why me?" But those moments will shape you. They will teach you lessons you didn't know you needed. They will make you resilient, brave, and unbreakable, just like all the women who came before you. You are their wildest dream, even on the days you don't feel like it.

You are becoming the first in your family to accomplish many things, making your parents proud. You will build the career they dreamed for you, with benefits like health insurance, and you will have the financial stability you once dreamed of. You'll walk into spaces no one in your family has ever been. You'll hold degrees no one thought possible. You'll manage more responsibilities and money than you ever imagined. You will travel the world, like Japan, Italy and Australia, places your family has never been, and you will carry them with you in every step, every flight, every passport stamp. You'll see mountains, oceans, and cities that feel like dreams, and you'll remember exactly where you came from.

You know how Mom tells you not to ask for things and reminds you there is food at home por que no tiene dinero? One day, you'll have your own money to take her out to eat wherever she wants, and you'll go shopping together. You'll buy her new shoes, outfits and perfumes, the way she wanted to do for you.

So keep going. Lift your head. Believe in your worth, even when it feels hard. You will grow into a woman who is strong, proud, and full of love, for yourself, for your family, for the next generation, and for the little girl who never gave up. And remember: no matter the obstacles in front of you, you will find a way. And sometimes... the way will find you.

Con mucho amor,
Rosario del futuro

WHERE ARE THEY NOW

As this story closes, life continues unfolding for us. My mom's transplanted kidney stopped working, and she returned to dialysis, although this time around, it felt manageable since I knew what to expect. She moved into her own apartment, making it the first time in her life that she lived alone. She's a short drive away, and I continue to be her caregiver, taking her to doctors' appointments and pharmacy runs, and anything else she needs help with. In her free time, she enjoys gardening and crocheting.

My dad continues to live in the Bay Area with his long-term partner. He recently retired from work and enjoys a more relaxed, slower pace of life. In his free time, he enjoys spending time outdoors and running.

My brother finished his military service and started a new career in the government sector. His three children are all grown up now with their own hopes and dreams.

I began writing this book after I got married. My husband and I celebrated with a destination wedding in Mexico, surrounded by our families and friends—a moment that felt like something out of a dream and a beautiful reminder that dreams really do come true. In our free time, we love taking walks along the beach and exploring new destinations together.

I continued to build my career in public service in a management role, and along the way, I made it a priority to share my story with students and their parents. I want them to see that the obstacles they face can be overcome and that their dreams are possible, even when the path isn't clear. I am deeply passionate about mentoring other first-generation students and professionals early in their careers, offering guidance, encouragement, and practical advice to help them navigate challenges I once faced. Helping others discover their potential and supporting them as they take their first steps in education or the workforce has become one of the most meaningful parts of my life. Through these experiences, I hope to not only inspire others but also to create a ripple effect, empowering the next generation to believe in themselves, take up space, and pursue their goals with confidence.

ACKNOWLEDGEMENTS

First, thank you to my parents for their love and support in all my endeavors. You taught me about work ethic, sacrifice, and the value of education. All these lessons have helped shape who I am today. You showed me what perseverance looks like long before I had the language for it. You gave me the strength, values, and courage to keep going even when the path wasn't clear.

To my brother and my family, thank you for your constant support, encouragement, and belief in me. Your presence, patience, and encouragement have inspired me to always do better, not just for myself, but for those we love.

To my husband, thank you for your unwavering support, patience, and belief in me. From the moment I shared that I was writing this book, your excitement and encouragement reminded me that this dream was worth pursuing. You stood beside me through moments of doubt and long days of writing, always reminding me to keep going. Your support gave me the confidence to trust my voice and see this project through.

To my new family, thank you for welcoming me with open arms and for your constant encouragement. Your kindness, support, and genuine excitement for this book made this journey feel even more meaningful. Knowing I had your belief and support behind me gave me strength and reassurance along the way, and I am deeply grateful to be part of such a loving family.

To my friends and family, near and far, primas and primos, thank you for your constant support, encouragement, and shared excitement throughout this journey. Your belief in me, your messages, and your pride reminded me why this story mattered and gave me the motivation to keep going. I'm deeply grateful for the love and support that has always surrounded me.

To my abuelas, abuelos, and ancestors, thank you for helping shape the woman I am today. Your strength, sacrifices, and resilience created the foundation I stand on. Because of you, I carry values of perseverance, courage, and hope, and I honor your legacy in everything I do.

A special thank you to my book mentor and friend, Erica Alfaro. You have truly changed my life. Your guidance, belief in me, and constant encouragement throughout this journey gave me the confidence to trust my voice and share my story. You showed me what's possible for Latinas when we speak up, take up space, and tell our stories with courage. Thank you for paving the way and for reminding me that our voices matter.

Thank you to our writers' group for your support, encouragement, and shared wisdom throughout this process. Your feedback, honesty, and sense of community made this journey feel less isolating and reminded me that I wasn't walking this path alone.

To the mentors and educators, both those I have had the privilege of knowing and those I have yet to meet, thank you for reminding me that I belonged in spaces I once doubted. Thank you for seeing potential in me before I fully saw it in myself, for showing me what is possible, and for opening doors not just for me, but for so many in our community. Your impact reaches far beyond individual moments, and your work continues to create paths for others to follow.

To my fellow first-generation students, children of immigrants, and my community, thank you for sharing your stories, your courage, and your continued strength during challenging times. You keep reminding me that we are resilient and capable of creating our own paths even when the road is uncertain. Your perseverance inspires me every day, and your journeys give this work meaning.

Thank you to Davina and her team at Alegria Publishing, especially my editor, Anne Marie Wells, for helping me bring this project to light. Your guidance, support, and expertise turned my vision into reality, and I am deeply grateful for all the care and dedication you poured into this book.

And to you, the reader—especially if you've ever felt the weight of expectation, responsibility, or loneliness—thank you for being here. I hope these pages help you feel seen, understood, and encouraged to trust yourself. If my story reminds you that your journey matters and that you can find a way forward, then this book has done what it was meant to do.

ABOUT THE AUTHOR

Rosario Aranda is a first-generation Latina, daughter of immigrants, mentor, and public speaker who learned the power of sacrifice, perseverance, and faith early on. Raised by parents who worked tirelessly to create opportunities they never had, Rosario grew up carrying both their dreams and her own.

She earned her bachelor's degree in communication and her master's degree in public administration while balancing work, family responsibilities, and caregiving. Her journey shaped a deep commitment to service, leadership, and mentoring others who are navigating similar challenges.

Today, Rosario is a mentor, public speaker, and workshop facilitator who supports daughters and children of immigrants through honest storytelling, leadership conversations, and meditation. She creates spaces for reflection, healing, and empowerment, reminding others that even when the path is unclear, they can and will find a way.

Rosario invites readers to continue the conversation through her speaking engagements, workshops, and community spaces, where she shares tools for building resilience, cultivating self-worth, and discovering purpose.